THE APPLAUSE ACTING SERIES

□ □ □ □ □ □ □ □ □ □ □ □

Edited by Maria Aitken

ACTING IN FILM
An Actor's Take on Movie Making

by

MICHAEL CAINE

THEATRE BOOK PUBLISHERS

An Applause Original
ACTING IN FILM
By Michael Caine

Copyright © 1990 by Applause Theatre Book Publishers
All rights reserved.

Library of Congress Cataloging-In-Publication Data

Caine, Michael.
    Acting in film: an actor's take on movie making / by Michael
Caine; edited by Maria Aitken.
      p.   cm. — (The Applause acting series)
    Includes bibliographical references.
    ISBN 0-936839-86-4   ISBN 1-55783-124-6 (pbk)
      ISBN 1-55783-034-7 (videocassette)
    1. Motion picture acting. I. Aitken, Maria. II. Title.
III. Series.
PN1995.9.A26C35   1990
791.43'028—dc20   89-39932
                                                  CIP

APPLAUSE THEATRE BOOK PUBLISHERS
211 W. 71st Street   406 Vale Road
New York, NY 10023   Tonbridge KENT TN9 1XR
(212) 595-4735 fax (212) 721-2856   0732 357755 fax 0732 770219

First Applause Printing, 1990

Second Applause Printing, 1990

Third Applause Printing, 1991

First Applause Paperback Printing, 1993

CONTENTS

ACTING IN FILM
An Actor's Take on Movie Making

DEATHTRAP
Directed by Sidney Lumet.   Warner Brothers, 1982.

Movie Acting: An Introduction

"If your concentration is total and
your performance is truthful,
you can lean back and the camera
will catch you every time;
it will never let you fall."

The ordinary man in the street doesn't get up in the morning and say to himself, "How shall I act today? What impression shall I give?" He just lives his life, goes about his business thinking his thoughts. A film actor must be sufficiently in charge of his material and in tune with the life of his character to think his character's most private thoughts as though no one were watching him—no camera spying on him. The camera just happens to be there. They say you've learned a foreign language when you start dreaming it. A film actor must be able to dream another person's dreams before he can call that character his own.

The first time you go out in front of a camera is not like going out on a first date. You don't have to make a special impression. The camera doesn't have to be wooed; the camera already loves you deeply. Like an attentive mistress, the camera hangs on your every word, your every look; she can't take her eyes off you. She is listening to and recording everything you do, however minutely you do it; you have never known such devotion. She is also the most faithful lover, while you, for most of your career, look elsewhere and ignore her.

If this amorous relationship with the camera makes movie acting sound easy, think again. Behaving realistically and truthfully in front of a camera is an exacting craft, one that requires steadfast discipline and application. Film acting was never easy, but during the past 30 years, this craft has become even more demanding, partly because of changes in technology, partly because of the requirements actors and directors have placed on themselves, and partly because of shifts in audience expectations.

If you catch somebody "acting" in a movie, that actor is doing it wrong. The moment he's caught "performing" for the camera, the actor has blown his cover. He's no longer a private character in a private world. Now he's a highly paid actor on contract to speak these lines for the public. Good-bye illusion. Good-bye career.

In the early talkies, actors came to the movies from a theatre tradition and, not surprisingly, they performed in a way that was designed for the theatre. They didn't just talk—they delivered orations as if to the last rows of the balcony. No one seemed to tell them that there was no balcony. To some extent this highly theatrical performing was necessary because the microphone was completely stationary in those days. The mike, in fact, was generally stuck in a bunch of flowers in the middle of a table, so if

A SHOCK TO THE SYSTEM
Directed by Jan Egleson.   Corsair Pictures, 1990.
Pictured with Elizabeth McGovern.

the actors moved away from the table, they had to raise their voices. But the technology is infinitely more sophisticated now. These days, microphones can be hidden under a shirt collar or in the fold of a dress and can catch an actor's softest whisper. There is no need for an actor to raise his voice artificially. In fact, he must do just the opposite.

PLAY FOR THE MOMENT;
IMMORTALITY WILL TAKE CARE OF ITSELF

The style of acting has changed, too. In the old days, if an actor had to cry in a scene, he'd launch into a big emotional number to show the audience his grief. He would probably base his performance on what he'd seen other actors doing in acclaimed performances. Whether that method was effective or not, it was the tradition of the times.

The modern film actor knows that real people in real life struggle *not* to show their feelings. It is more truthful, and more potent, to fight against the tears, only yielding after all those defense mechanisms are exhausted. If today's actor emulates film, he'd be better off watching a documentary. The same is true of drunkenness. In real life, a drunk makes a huge effort to appear sober. A coarsely acted stage or film drunk reels all over the place to show you he's drunk. It's artificial. And eventually, that kind of acting puts up a barrier between the actor and the audience, so that nothing the character says or does will be believed. Credibility becomes an issue; and once an issue, it is never overcome. In other words, screen acting

THE IPCRESS FILE
Directed by Sidney J. Furie.   Universal, 1965.

today is much more a matter of "being" than "performing."

Audiences themselves have had a lot to do with the changes in film acting. They catch on very fast to what is truthful and what is not. Once audiences saw acting like Henry Fonda's in *The Grapes of Wrath*, they tuned in to the difference between behavior that is based on carefully observed reality and the stagier, less convincing stuff. Marlon Brando's work in *On the Waterfront* was so relaxed and underplayed, it became another milestone in the development of film acting. Over the years, the modern cinema audience has been educated to watch for and catch the minute signals that an actor conveys. By wielding the subtlest bit of body language, the actor can produce an enormously powerful gesture on the screen. In *The Caine Mutiny*, the novel's author tells us that Captain Queeg plays nervously with two steel balls in his hand. In the film, Humphrey Bogart knew that most of the time, just the click of those balls on the sound track was all the audience would need—he didn't even have to *look* neurotic.

THE CAMERA WILL CATCH YOU EVERY TIME

The close-up is the shot on which film relies most when it comes to transmitting the subtleties of emotion and thought. It can give an actor tremendous power, but that potential energy requires enormous concentration to be realized. The close-up camera won't mysteriously transform a drab moment into something spectacular unless the actor has found something spectacular in the moment. In fact it will do just the opposite: the close-up camera will seek out the tiniest uncertainty and magnify it. "Drying" (forgetting your lines) can be covered up on stage, where the actor is perhaps twenty feet from the front row of the audience; but the camera will betray the smallest unscheduled hesitation. If a member of the crew walks across my eye-line, off camera, when I'm doing a close-up, I immediately ask for a retake. I may not have thought my concentration lapsed—the director may assure me everything is fine—but the camera will have caught that minute flicker at the back of my eyes.

If your concentration is total and your performance is truthful, you can lean back and the camera will catch you every time; it will never let you fall. It's watching you. It's your friend. Remember, it loves you. It listens to and records everything you do, no matter how minutely you do it. If theatre acting is an operation with a scalpel, movie acting is an operation with a laser.

The scale of a film performance may be smaller than that of a performance in the theatre, but the intensity is just as great. Perhaps greater. On stage you have the dramatic thrust of the whole play to help you along. In film you shoot isolated moments, probably in the wrong sequence, and you have to constantly crank yourself up to an intense pitch of concentration on every shot. There isn't any coasting along in films; your brain is basically working double time or you don't exist on the screen. And you would be surprised how large a "small" performance can be on film, provided it is rooted in

BILLION DOLLAR BRAIN
Directed by Ken Russell.   United Artists, 1967.

naturalism. But don't just stand there and do nothing; and it won't help to make semaphore signals the way you do in the theatre. Don't imagine that you do everything theatrically but just at a reduced pitch, either. You must be thinking every moment because the camera looks into your mind, and the audience sees what the camera sees. The real key is in your mental transmission. If the mind is in overdrive, the body is headed in the right direction.

LESS IS MORE

I sometimes encounter actors who think they're going

to steal a scene by being big and bombastic. Those actors are using their bodies and voices instead of their brains. They don't realize that in terms of voice and action, less is more. You see the great theatre actor who can't be bothered to come to terms with the movie medium. He probably needs a new Mercedes, so he's condescended to cope with a cinema gig between productions of *Titus Andronicus*. Now put the camera on him. Watch. Everyone goes into hysterics. The voice is too loud, the movements—famous for causing whole theatre audiences to gasp—now seem suddenly exaggerated and false. If I'm playing opposite somebody who goes into orbit like that, I just come in underneath him. I stick to the naturalism I believe in, and he is left up there looking pretty stupid.

A tree is a tree in the movies. It's not that painted bit of canvas that says, "We're in the theatre. We've agreed to suspend disbelief and pretend it's not all cardboard. We're going to see wonderful stage actors *acting*." On stage, you have to project your voice or the words will sink without a trace into the third row of seats. On stage, the basic premise is action; you have to sell your attitudes to the audience. In movies, the microphone can always hear you, no matter how softly you speak, no matter where the scene is taking place. In movies, it is *reaction* that gives every moment its potency. That's why listening in films is so important, as well as the use of the eyes in the close-up. You don't have to shout and scream. You don't ever have to do it big.

SCREEN POTENTIAL

It is impossible to tell someone's screen potential by just looking at him. Nobody knows what the secret ingredient is, and until you see an actor on the screen doing his work, you can't tell what's going to happen. There are just some fortunate people out there whom you, I and millions of other people want to look at. Look at the old screen tests of Marilyn Monroe and James Dean—those tests reveal a lot of fear; but they also reveal that magical stuff that dream movie careers are made of.

The screen test is the basic initial assessment of your screen potential and it can be rough. Most screen tests are done with another actor—not one of the stars (who hasn't time to try out novices) but someone specially hired for the event. They put the camera on you and do a close-up. They turn you sideways to get a look at your profile. Then they pick out one of the more difficult dialogue scenes from the picture for which you're auditioning and tell you to do that scene with the back-of-the-head actor. Your screen potential is judged by what you look like, how relaxed you are, the sound of your voice, and by that rare hard-to-define commodity that radiates from some movie actors like gold and diamonds.

GET YOUR OWN ACT TOGETHER

Film acting makes other demands, mental and physical, that never show up in the final results and are hard to imagine unless you've at least played a small part for a day or two. These demands start at home, before you even get in front of the camera. Much of the preparation sounds like getting ready for school rather than entering the glamorous world of film, but then you don't actually find glamor on the film set, just lots of hard work.

First, you have to psych yourself into a good night's sleep, after having arranged a fool proof wake-up call. Second, you have to be sure of your transportation arrangements when you do get up in the morning because your time is their money, and if you don't know how you are getting to the studio or the location on time, you won't have the job when you do get there, late. Establish where to go (the venue of your shoot might always be changing) and then mentally rehearse your journey there as if it were the first scene in the film. You've got to get your own act together before the camera's act can begin. Being prepared isn't just for the demands of your part; it's also for the demands of the studio or location. You must get your bearings and establish where to go and what to do when you get there.

Once you're on location, any neurotic fussing distracts attention from the main event, which is the making of a movie. You have to be ready—that is, in your makeup and in costume—at dawn. Now you're all dressed up with nowhere to go. Careful. Don't dribble butter down your chin or trail your trouser bottoms in the mud. Don't waste energy with a lot of frenzied socializing, either, even though you may find yourself waiting all day before you are called to do anything. And don't expect regular meal breaks; you may have to keep shooting so that the camera people can catch the light they want. No one will be deliberately trying to starve you; you may even be able to smell the canteen around the corner, but as with everyone else, that film is your first and only priority. Even your stomach only grumbles on cue.

PLAYS ARE PERFORMED; MOVIES ARE MADE

Shooting a movie is a long, relentless grind. If you're not physically strong, if you don't have the stamina to go the distance, don't bother starting the race. There may be night shooting and you may have to be back on location at dawn the next morning to start all over again. Waiting can be as tiring as doing, but you've got to save the best of yourself for when the camera rolls. Then, when it does, be ready and able to give not merely the best you've got, but give precisely what the director wants, sometimes under demanding working conditions: in lousy weather, wearing a crippling costume, and mobbed by distracting crowds who can't tear themselves away from this fascinating event on their doorstep.

The single most startling principle to grasp for the theatre actor entering the world of film for the first time is that not only have you got to know your lines on day one, you will also have directed yourself to play them in a certain way. And all this accomplished *without* necessarily discussing the role with the director, *without* meeting the other people in the cast, *without* rehearsal on the set. The stage actor is used to slowly wading into the play's reality. First a read-through with the assembled cast to acquaint

CALIFORNIA SUITE
Directed by Herbert Ross.   Columbia, 1978.

him with the broad outline of the author's intentions. Then the director's view. Then maybe a free-for-all discussion. Gradually, book in hand, stage actors splash themselves with gentle doses of the play, scene by scene, starting with Act One, Scene One. Pity the poor stage actor who is about to be immersed, Baptist style, in the movies. Plays are performed. Movies are made.

There may be rehearsals, but that is by no means certain; and more than likely, if you have them, they won't be for you but for the benefit of the camera people! And despite all your preparation, you have to remain flexible. You might have to incorporate new lines or physical changes at a moment's notice. Panic is prohibited.

It's very tough for the theatre actor to understand that the other actors' performances aren't really his business. Whether he is helped or hindered by the other actors' performances in the shot, he must react as if they have given him exactly what he wants, even if he feels shortchanged. Remember, unless you are actually looking through the camera and seeing the shot, you can never know if all the performers are delivering the goods or not. Half the time, movie acting is so subtle that the actors on the set with me will say:

"I don't know what you're doing."

And I say, "Wait till you see the rushes." (Sometimes I've even said that to the director.)

Once a director said to me: "I didn't see that,

Michael. I didn't see that on the take."

And I said, "Where were you sitting?"

"Over there."

So I said, "How do you expect to have seen anything? The lens is over here by me."

Another tough challenge for a theatre actor presents itself when he has to summon up an actor who isn't there—that is, talk to the camera with no actor behind it. Mostly the off-camera actor *is* there and will be very generous with his time and give you just as intense a performance as he did in his close-up; but sometimes he's needed elsewhere and you have to cope by pretending he's there when he isn't. At this point, I don't care if he's there or not—in fact, I usually suggest he go home. I could do it to the wall because I hang on to the emotional memory of how it was in the shot when he *was* there. The only completely disconcerting moment occurs when the continuity girl stands in for a passionate bit and drones away, "I - love - you - darling - but - I - have - been - unfaithful," and you have to emote away, "Oh, God, no! Please don't!" That's a bit difficult.

Discipline is necesssary at any level of film acting, but in some ways, small parts are the hardest. It's terrifying to have to say just one line. I did it in about a hundred pictures. I played a police constable in *The Day the Earth Caught Fire*, for instance. I had to hold up the traffic, direct cars in one direction, trucks in another, and say my ONE BIG LINE. When finally I thought I knew what I was supposed to be doing, and the director obligingly said "Action!" inevitably the police helmet came right down over my eyes! I couldn't see where to direct the trucks and I couldn't remember my line. The director said to me: "You will never work again." (By the way, there are some things you never say in the movie business: that's one of them. It usually turns out that the person who says it never works again.) The point is that reliability is at a premium in films. And reliability isn't only punctuality or making sure your shoes stay shined. Reliability is also functioning well under pressure when the camera rolls. Just to come out even against everything that's flung at you requires a high level of alert competence. I let that police helmet distract me.

"QUIET!" AND YOU'VE NEVER HEARD SUCH QUIET

And in the midst of your necessary alertness, let's not forget that you have to achieve relaxation. Movie acting *is* relaxation. If you're knocking yourself out, you're doing it wrong. So one of the first things you have to learn is how to overcome nerves. Preparation is a big step toward controlling those nerves. All the work you do beforehand is going to help subdue the fear. All your preparation points come together to create a safety net. And everybody needs one. Remember: in film acting, you don't usually know the director's intentions until you get on the set, and terror may strike the best of us under those circumstances. There's the big director and his big star; they and everybody else are all waiting poised for you to come up with this great thing that you're paid so highly to do. There's the moment when they say "Quiet!"

and you've never heard such quiet. It's deafening. You can hear the blood in your own eardrums. Then the director says "Action!" If you're not experienced, that moment turns you into a sort of nervous automaton.

The social situation doesn't help much, either, particularly if you're the new guy and the movie's been shooting for a while. Everybody's saying, "Hello, Charlie. How ya doin? Get me a cup of tea . . . " And you're standing there not knowing anybody. Then over comes your star—usually a pain in the neck, a bit conceited, and doesn't talk to you because you've only got a small part—and you stand there, nervewracked. It's especially scary if there's a big scene going on and you have the last line—your only line.

It's no wonder I have sympathy for one-line actors. I've been there. The troops come down the hill, the beach explodes, and you say:

"Quick! The Germans are *crumming*!" (One line!)

"Who got this guy?!"

The casting director comes in and says, "What's the matter?"

"This guy can't say one line!"

(You're standing there cursing yourself.)

"All those troops have to come over the hill again!" (Because of my *crumming* line!) "It'll take two hours to put the explosives back in . . ."

Then the great star says his long speech absolutely

perfectly, yet again; and you say:

"Quick! The Germans are *crumming*!" Then you ask desperately, "Can we post-synch that? Will it be all right?"

And the director says, "NO! We've got to do it again!"

Preparation

"You're your first best audience long before anybody else hears you. So don't be an easy audience. Keep asking for more."

So to avoid all that horror, *prepare*. Apart from anything else, preparation uses up a lot of the nervous energy that otherwise might rise up to betray you. Channel that energy; focus it into areas that you control.

The first step in preparation is to learn your lines until saying them becomes a predictable reflex. And don't mouth them silently; say them aloud until they become totally your property. Hear yourself say them, because the last thing you want is the sound of your own voice taking you by surprise or not striking you as completely convincing. If you can't convince yourself, the chances are that you won't convince the character opposite you, or the director. You're your first best audience long before anybody else hears you. So don't be an easy audience. Keep asking for more.

I learn lines on my own; I never have anyone read. Nevertheless, I try to learn lines as dialogue, as logical replies to what someone else has said or as a logical response to a situation. You'll never find me going down

THE ISLAND
Directed by Michael Ritchie.   Universal, 1980.
Pictured with Jeffrey Frank.

the page with an envelope, blocking out my own speech and revealing the one before because it then becomes nothing more than "cues" and "speeches." If you haven't grasped the logic of why you say a particular thing, you won't say it properly or convincingly. And if your thoughts aren't linked to what you're saying, then you won't be able to say a line as if you invented it on the spot. So you must be familiar with the whole conversation, not just your own bits. One of the most crucial jobs you'll have as an actor will be to know what you're thinking when you're not talking.

Say your lines aloud while you're learning them until you find what strikes you as the best possible expression of that particular thought. If there are plausible variations, develop them, practice them, too; but keep them up your sleeve. If the director rejects your brilliant interpretation, you're not left in a blank state of horror. You've already imagined and prepared other reactions to demonstrate. And most important, you've allowed for some element of malleability in your performance. Give your best reading as if it were the only one possible; but your mind should be hanging loose enough to take a leap, if necessary. For the moment, go with the line readings that seem to you the most valid. It may take some doing, but once the thought process is right, the words will follow.

So much of it really is a matter of repetition, of saying the lines over and over again until you're sick of them; until someone can give you a cue, and you can say, feel, and react to the whole cycle of events, including those related to everyone else's parts. That confidence is your safeguard against terror. Otherwise, in the tension of the close-up, when you're standing there and someone is saying, "Quiet! Turn over! Speed! Action!" you may well go, "To bum or not to bim, that is the question!"

Learn your lines for the whole film before you start shooting, and keep studying them during the gaps in your shooting. I was once caught on the hop when I was filming *Kidnapped*. We were shooting on the Isle of Mull. The weather conditions were perfect and we were ahead of schedule. Things were going so brilliantly that the director, Delbert Mann, came up to me at lunchtime and said:

"It's such great weather, I want to shoot your last scene this afternoon."

My last scene was a two-page soliloquy about Scotland and what it meant to me. I hadn't prepared a word. I stared at him and said, "It's not on the schedule for today."

Mann said, "We'll never get a better day than this one."

I said, "Give me an hour." Somehow I did it and I did it in one take. But I would have saved myself a lot of sweat if I had made it my business to familiarize myself with all my lines before I started shooting the film.

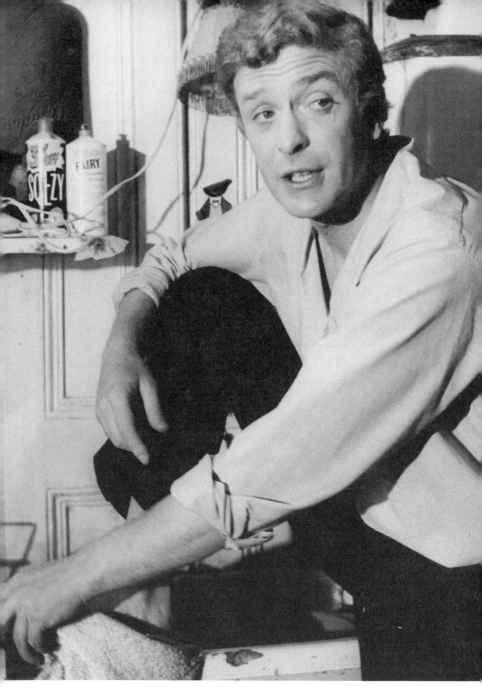

ALFIE
Directed by Lewis Gilbert.   Paramount, 1966.

TIME IS ONLY DEAD IF YOU KILL IT

There is a lot of dead time for an actor during the making of a movie. You can sleep and possibly appear dopey on camera, or you can socialize and wear yourself out. I socialize enough not to offend anyone, but I deliberately spend a lot of time in the dressing room. I use the time to go through those lines. Unoccupied time doesn't have to be dead time. It's only dead if you kill it. A lot of actors run other businesses from their dressing rooms or trailers. I was working with Sylvester Stallone and I asked him what was so attractive about his trailer that he kept rushing back to it between takes. I thought he might have a girl in there. "I'm writing *Rocky III*" he said. Then there was an actor who used to play the New York Stock Exchange from his trailer. He's not a film actor anymore; but I saw him on television: he has his own program about stocks and shares. I figure it's more profitable for me to deal with the business at hand because if I play my part right, the current picture may make more money for me than any other business. If an actor is thinking about another business, maybe he should *be* in another business.

I'll tell you what goes on in my trailer. Show business. Walk in and you'll see me doing a scene over and over again. There I am mumbling it and mumbling it and still mumbling it, so that it becomes second nature. It's no good if you're about to start a take and you're thinking, "It's coming soon, that difficult bit where I say 'One hundred and thirty-eight North Ponders End Road SW16.'" You must be able to stand there *not* thinking of that line.

You take it off the other actor's face. He is presumably new-minting the dialogue as if he himself just thought of it by listening and watching, as if it were all new to him, too. Otherwise, for your next line, you're not listening and not free to respond naturally, to act spontaneously.

THOUGHT RECOGNITION

It may sound like a contradiction, but you achieve spontaneity on the set through preparation of the dialogue at home. As you prepare, find ways of making your responses appear newly minted, not preprogrammed. In life, we often pick up the thought that provokes our next remark halfway through someone else's speech. Thoughts don't leap to the mouth automatically. We don't interrupt at every occasion when a thought formulates itself; or, if we do, we don't have many friends. Similarly, in a film script, your internal thought processes might well start articulating themselves long before you get the chance to speak. The script sometimes directs you to interrupt, but if it doesn't, your thought may start well before you get a chance to respond. There may be a key word that triggers you during the sentence the other actor is saying. So pick up on that; form your thought and be ready to speak. For example:

Other Actor: I've got to get a bus to Clapham—I'm already late for my date.

You: You won't get far. There's a bus strike.

The other actor doesn't stop talking after he says "bus," so you can't get in and say your line at the actual moment of thought recognition. But when you hear the

By courtesy of the Rank Organization PLC.

KIDNAPPED
Directed by Delbert Mann.   AIP, 1971.

key word "bus," from that point on you know what you're going to say directly after he stops. You can show this by your reaction. And that bit of acting can only come from serious listening.

Or you can bring new life to an apparently mundane reply by planning a thought process based on a key word and then never voicing it:

Other Actor: Would you like some tea?

You: Yes, please.

"Tea" is the key word. The simple word "tea" can open up so many responses. Let's say you would have preferred coffee. The minute the other actor says "tea," your eyes will change because you'd really like coffee. Or maybe you're allergic to tea. Then you answer politely, but with a bit of anguish, knowing that you won't really drink it. The camera thrives on niceties like that; yet you often see actors missing out on these little presents that can open up whole realms of possible reaction. "Tea" could be an indication that he's too poor to offer you booze, or that he regards you as an alcoholic who shouldn't be offered a drink. Take the script and explore these possibilities because to pick up key words opens a repertoire of potential response that can lift a scene off the page and into reality. Don't make a fetish of it or you will complicate things unnecessarily. You'll seem a maniac if *everything* sets you off. But take it to reasonable bounds and you'll find that your performance is more interesting to you and more believable on the screen.

MINIATURE GOLF

There may or may not be rehearsals; it depends entirely on the director. So you must do as much as you can to construct your role before you get on the set. The director always expects you to bring a fully formed characterization with you, and this without your seeing the set or meeting fellow actors. Make the decisions about

your character's physical mannerisms, practice them—
and keep it simple. Once you get on the set, you will have
to repeat those mannerisms and actions accurately for a
variety of shots.

We'll deal with special problems of continuity later,
but basically you usually need to repeat a sequence at least
three times on film: once for the long shot, once for the
medium shot, and once for the close-up. The long shot is
the wide-angle shot taken at a distance. This shot reveals
all the ingredients of a scene. If there are three actors
practicing their golf strokes on the office carpet, in the
long shot you will see all of them plus the carpet. This
shot is also frequently called the "master shot" because it
shows the whole scene. It is the best guide to the
placement of the camera for the other shots and it is the
reference for inclusion of other shots when the scene is
edited. The medium shot is a closer view of selected
ingredients. The close-up is a very close view of only one
element. If you were one of the golfers, the close-up
might be of your feet on the carpet or of your face.

When you prepare your character's physical
mannerisms or actions at home, keep them simple, so that
later, on the set, you can repeat them accurately for each
type of shot. If you fiddle around with your golf club
during the master shot, you must fiddle in exactly the
same way for the other shots. Initiating a movement that
you cannot repeat will often mean that scenes will have to
be shot again. If you are holding the putter on your left
side for a particular line in the master, but you shift it to

your right for the medium shot (which may be filmed several hours later), then when the editor comes to cut the film he won't be able to use that shot. It would look as if the golf club had jumped around of its own accord.

You've learned your lines, now it's time to learn the layout of the set and begin to orient yourself to your surroundings. I go through each scene and do my actions the same way, over and over, exactly as I imagine I will have to do them on the set. Wherever I happen to be, whether at home or in a hotel room, I rearrange the furniture and try to put tables and chairs in places that create a logical mock-up of the scene. I put out cups and saucers or whatever I may need and I time the dialogue around my actions. Now obviously you may not know the exact layout of the set you will be working on or the exact nature of the props you will be given to use, but any clear decision you can make beforehand will provide you with a life raft. Somehow it's a lot easier to change one well-planned course of action for another precise course of action than to turn a vague idea about physical movement into a concrete one on the spur of the moment. And it's surprising how many of your assumptions about furniture and props will turn out to be right.

Plan your mannerisms and actions precisely and keep them simple so that you can repeat them effortlessly and accurately. But don't overdo it. This is not the area for inspired improvisation. Keep it simple with those golf clubs. If you're going to initiate an action, PLAN IT. Organize your physical actions and tasks so that they are logical—that way you will remember to do them—and practice them so that they remain memorable. You have got to be able to do a physical task the same way over and over again absolutely perfectly. Otherwise, the master shot, the medium shot, and the close-up *will not match*, scenes will have to be shot again, and you will be costing the producers time and money, not the most endearing quality for producers to remember when they're casting their next film.

At the
Studio
or
On Location

"It's vital that an actor never
hold anything up
for any reason he can avoid."

Time is money and it's vital that an actor never hold anything up for any reason he can avoid. On arrival at the studio or location, it's up to you to get the hang of the geography as soon as possible. Find your dressing room, the makeup and hairdressing department, and the shooting stage or location. You probably spoke with an assistant director when you got your call to appear on the set; make sure you introduce yourself to him, if he hasn't already run you to earth, because it's his job to summon you to the set at the appropriate moment. Always wait to be summoned. Eager hanging-about before you are called is *not* recommended. Everybody on a film set has a function, and if you don't, you're probably in the way.

The first port-of-call is makeup and hairdressing—a department where everyone is trained to make you as happy and relaxed as possible. Obviously you have already thought about the way your character should look. If your part is large enough, you will have had prior discussion with the director and with makeup and hair artists. If your part doesn't measure up to that kind of attention, the director will have already given that department some indication of what he wants. These guys are experts, so unless you're related to Max Factor it's best to let them get on with it. Besides, the makeup and hairdressing department is usually the hub of the universe, socially speaking, and word of your behavior there soon spreads.

If you're feeling particularly sensitive about the bags under your eyes or the pimple on your chin, go on, point that out. If you're fair and have blond eyelashes, as I have, you ask for mascara (because if you're in a movie and you have blond eyelashes, you might as well be in a radio play). Eyes are what eventually sell you in a film. But makeup will most likely have spotted that problem anyway.

Once the makeup and hairdressing artists are done with you, it's up to you to try to preserve the effect. No one wants this expensive handiwork ruined. Don't immediately eat a greasy hamburger or walk in the rain; someone will be there with an umbrella—wait for him! Also, begin to take careful note of variations that may inadvertently occur in your look or costume between scenes: a change of hairstyle, the addition of a coat of nail varnish, etc. Polaroids will be taken on the set to ensure that your appearance remains consistent day after day. Makeup artists and directors will usually take note of any inconsistencies, but no one is infallible and no one is going to thank you if a scene has to be reshot because you held your tongue. When I was in *Zulu*, my first major role, I had a scene that required me to jump off a burning

SLEUTH
Directed by Joseph L. Mankiewicz.   20th Century-Fox, 1972.

house. Massed Zulus were coming toward me. It was a big number. We finally finished the scene, much to my relief. Then the continuity girl suddenly said, "Hang on. Michael's shirt was buttoned up to the collar in the sequence before this and now he's got two buttons undone." Of course I'd undone them between takes, probably because of the heat. We had to shoot the whole damn thing over again.

The costume that was fitted for you with the costume designer will be in your dressing room or trailer when you arrive, and a wardrobe assistant will check with you to make sure that the costume is complete and that it fits properly. But as with your makeup and hair, taking care of the costume until you get on the set is up to you. Common sense comes in here. If you're supposed to be immaculate, it doesn't make sense to sit about in the clothes for hours because you'll just be a crumpled mess when your moment comes. But if it's a lived-in sort of costume, it may be a good idea to get into it ahead of time. If it's a period costume, you may also want to wear it for a while to get the hang of a cloak or train. These decisions are up to you; the only definite rule is to be ready when you are called to the set. The assistant director will warn you in plenty of time.

I always think I'm ready, but I've got a psychological aversion to getting my tie or shoes on. When the moment comes to be all dressed I sometimes discover the shoes are the wrong size, and then there's a big panic while the dresser rushes off to find another pair. While my shot is being lined up, I'm usually knotting my tie and still wearing my own shoes. I try to wear my own until the last minute because they're bound to be more comfortable. In fact, I always ask if my feet are going to be in a shot; the director usually tells me, "No, it's fine," and then the camera pulls back and, lo and behold, there are my dirty old sneakers. If I'm playing a well-dressed businessman, the shooting has to stop while the right shoes are produced. So don't follow my practice on this one.

TRY EVERYTHING

There is some sleuth work you can do at the studio that will add considerably to your command of your role. In fact, if you don't do it, you may very well look like an idiot once you do get on the set. If that set is supposed to be your character's home or office, you'd better get out there before it's filled with technicians and learn where every prop and piece of furniture is and how everything works. I always go onto the set before the take so that I won't have to look around to find the cigarette box when I reach for that cigarette or the phone when it rings. Those things should be second nature, as they are in your own home or office. Make sure you know which way each door opens because you're supposed to have been in and out of that room fifteen hundred times. If you try to leave your house by pushing a door that only opens inward, or show any hesitation at all, it's obvious that you're really not at home there. You've got to know how every object on that set works because in your own home, you do everything with extra facility.

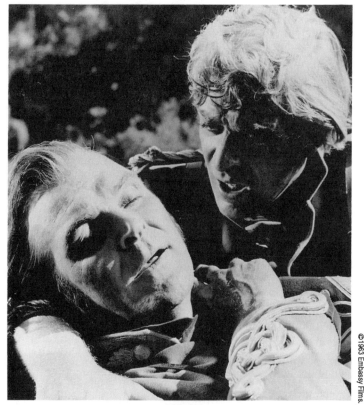

ZULU
Directed by Cy Endfield. Embassy Films, 1963.
Pictured with Stanley Baker.

Doors are always a problem on a set and especially worth a thorough check ahead of time. If you have to knock on a door and then enter, you may find when you try the knob that the paint that has just dried has glued the door shut. During the rehearsal, try *everything* you are supposed to use or handle, and if there isn't a rehearsal, try it all on your own anyway. So if the door is stuck, you can politely inform the assistant director and he can get one of the crew to solve the problem. Of course, now here comes the take: you knock on the door, and it flies open before you even touch the knob. That's typical. But at least you did all *you* could.

The way the set is put together sometimes surprises you during fights, too. You don't fight full blast in rehearsal, of course, so on the take, while you're swinging a punch past the other guy's head, you may find your fist going right through the castle wall that's supposed to be centuries old and three feet thick.

Just the opposite applies to sets that aren't supposed to be your own home or office (or your mother's home or girlfriend's office)—that is, somewhere you supposedly have never been before. Let it surprise you. In the event of retakes, try to remember that initial sense of disorientation and recreate it. Anticipation is the enemy of all actors. It wreaks particularly savage havoc in films because the camera sees *everything*, especially lack of spontaneity.

GAMBIT
Directed by Ronald Neame.   Universal, 1966.

In Front
of the
Camera —
Before
You Shoot

"In film, other actors' performances really are not your concern. If the other actor isn't giving you what you want, act as though he were."

Always tell everyone your first name when you're at the studio or location, because if you insist on being called Mister, Miss, or Ms., you might find hammers and lamps falling off the catwalk perilously close to your head. The sooner you establish a friendly relationship with the technical people, the sooner they'll go out of their way to help you. No one despises inexperience, only toffee-nosed inexperience. Don't establish friendliness by moving your own props or being helpful in a technical vein, however, or you'll run into union problems; each technician has a clearly defined job that he alone is supposed to do. And always, especially if you're concerned with looking beautiful on screen, be nice to the cameraman because he can make or break you. Most of them wouldn't do anything too detrimental because they want their work to be respected. And of course when I say "be nice" I mean be cordial, say good morning nicely; I'm not advising you to bribe him or throw your clothes off and hurl yourself at him. But if you want to look really handsome or beautiful, good manners do help.

SLEUTH
Directed by Joseph L. Mankiewicz.   20th Century-Fox, 1972.
Pictured with Laurence Olivier.

In movies, the form of rehearsals depends entirely on the director. But since the director's mind is on all aspects of the film, don't expect any particular accolade or sign of approval during rehearsals. If your director isn't saying anything to you, that means your work is probably fine. In theatre, actors and director use rehearsals to explore character and relationships. In film, at this point in the process, there isn't time for dissection of your role. You use rehearsals to show the director and other actors what you're proposing to do physically and more or less how you're going to say the lines; you use rehearsals to show the thorough preparation that you've been hired for.

Usually rehearsals are used to set blocking, which is the process of working out the moves for each scene. Don't be cowed by technical considerations here; the actor's instinct is vital to this process. Move where and how you feel it is comfortable and right for the role, because they can put the camera on top of St. Paul's Cathedral, if necessary, to suit your moves. Of course, if the director says, "I want you to end up on that spot, no matter *how* you feel about it," then you had better follow his instructions and get there.

PRACTICE WITH DANGER AND YOU LOSE IT

Do not use rehearsals to give your all as an actor. In theatre, a director will often encourage you to get to performance level well before opening night. In film, it's no good hitting those high notes before the take because film acting is about danger. If you practice with danger, you lose it. If you rehearse a risk, it is no longer a risk. You also deprive the other actor of his spontaneous response to that extra something you are going to zing in there when the camera rolls. You should only take that ultimate risk, provide that real surprise, when someone says "action." Then, by all means, push yourself a little further than you want to go.

In theatre, it's natural to worry about what the other actors are giving you on stage because an important part of live theatre is that immediate give and take. But in film, other actors' performances really are not your concern. If the other actor isn't giving you what you want, act as though he were. If you feel the wrong actor has been cast in the part, recast him *in your mind*. Other actors may feel the same about you! Try to hang on to your contribution without being distracted. I know how difficult this is because the only time I ever "dry" is when I get over-fascinated by bad acting. But you really don't know what the director has in mind, and he's the guv'nor here. He may end up using all the shots of you reacting and just use the other fellow's part as a voice off camera. Or it may never have been his intention to have you both in the shot. Regardless of his original intention, he may change his mind during the editing. So always act and react as if you were getting the ideal response because you never know what's going to be used once the editing begins. The director's going to do what's best for the picture, and if you have been at your best, you may find that you get to be shown in the final cut.

When a scene is blocked to everyone's satisfaction, marks are made on the floor, or strategic twigs are placed on the ground if you are outdoors, or you will be required to line yourself up with a fixed object because you must end up either in that preordained spot or else be out of focus. Obviously an actor can't look down to see if he has hit his mark, so the way to ensure accuracy is to stand on the mark, then say your line at performance pace while walking backward to an earlier position. When you go forward from that earlier position, saying the same line,

HANNAH AND HER SISTERS
Directed by Woody Allen.   Orion, 1985.

you wind up on the mark. If you practice the rhythm of this a few times, you won't go wrong. You won't forget your line, either, because words and movement will be married in your head, like a song and dance.

THE STAND-IN

Once the blocking is fixed, the lighting technician goes to work. At this point, you get out of the way and a stand-in who has been watching your moves during rehearsal takes over. Sometimes lighting a scene can take an hour and a half to two hours, and no one expects the actor who's in the scene to stand there that long. My stand-in is usually a big 6'2" blond guy whose face is the same height from the floor as mine to ensure that when I get back on the set my face won't be in the dark. Stand-ins will sometimes get you a cup of coffee; my stand-in is a particular friend of mine. But stand-ins can on occasion send you rushing out to look at yourself in the mirror. I've been in movies now for close to twenty-seven years, and when I first started, they'd say, "This is your stand-in," and there'd be this great-looking young guy standing there. Eventually, one morning you come in and they say, "This is your stand-in," and there's this old fellow standing there with a bald head, wearing a wig.

In America, I've even had a woman stand-in. Now, in the States in particular, you get a lot of women in the cinema. The days of all-male crews are over. When I worked with Alan Alda, who's a great feminist, it was the first time I'd worked with a female first assistant director. I did a double take when I worked on a picture in Los Angeles and there was an electrician who looked just like Julie Christie. It was really strange to see this beautiful girl walking by, carrying a lamp, with great big muscles in her arms. Needless to say, she did a marvelous job.

The last event before you shoot is a final makeup and hair check. This is the part that the assistant director always tries to rush along because if people are self-indulgent, this can take up a lot of time. But, remember, it is *your* face up there on that screen, so be firm if you think you need attention. A good makeup artist will always be keeping a sharp eye on you anyway because, after all, it's their reputation up there as well.

RELAX AND BE NERVOUS

At this point, if you haven't prepared properly, your nerves may threaten to swamp you. But because you've reduced your fear of the unknown by preparing as much as possible, you should be left with a *healthy* amount of nervous energy—useful energy that can be channeled into performance. One way of releasing that nervous energy productively is to experiment with various relaxation and focusing exercises.

Here's a little number I do before a long take: take a slow deep breath in, then bend over and let your arms dangle, really relaxed. Straighten up slowly, breathing out gently and evenly. This exercise relaxes you, helps concentration and gives you control. If you are going to be shooting a scene where you need extra tuning up, just inhale and exhale quickly for a short time—it gets the oxygen to the brain. You feel and look like an absolute twit, panting away, but you find you get a rush to your head, your eyes begin to sparkle a bit, and you're ready to play an energetic scene, mental or physical. Just be careful not to overdo the panting or you will hyperventilate and pass out.

Usually I play the character who terrifies other people, so in *Sleuth*, it was rather an unfamiliar experience when my character thought he was going to be killed and was abjectly terrified himself. Instead of dealing with my natural nervousness about the scene, I purposely let my nerves take over. I was surprised at the extent of them. It was relatively simple to become a gibbering wreck. Larry Olivier knew immediately what was happening with me and played up to it, so on that occasion my fears helped me out. But the way I figure it, generally I need all the help I can get to calm down.

In film, you make your actions and reactions realities whenever you can. If you're supposed to be breathless from running, get breathless from running. On stage, technique can often fool an audience: you can *act* as though you are breathless from having run ten laps, you can drop a coffee cup and the audience will believe you are anxious. But in film, you cannot fool the camera with technique. If I've got a long sequence in which I'm supposed to be nervous, I avoid my relaxation ploys and go and drink a cup of coffee, which strings the nerves along. Drink two cups, and your hand will start to shake; five or six cups, and your lips will twitch.

But whether you're supposed to be tense or relaxed in a scene, hang on to the knowledge that everyone is there to get the greatest performance from you that you've ever given. Don't be intimidated by anyone. Everybody's on your side. They all want you to be great. I've produced movies and I can tell you that if I put you in a movie, I want you to be great, even more than you want to be great.

The electrician will scramble up on the catwalks to set the light so that there's no glint in your eye; you've got seventy or eighty people concentrating on getting your best face on that screen and helping you say the line right. You may think, "I've got to do something, otherwise I'm not going to be interesting." But if you can attain that basic relaxation, that's all you need. Just block everybody out and relax. No one's going to kill you; no one's going to upset you. Everything is being done to help you do it right, because film acting is bloody difficult work, and everybody knows that.

BEYOND THE POSEIDON ADVENTURE
Directed by Irwin Allen.   Warner Brothers, 1979.
Pictured with Sally Field.

The
Take

"Acting is not a competition;
everything must be done for the good
of the film or else everybody loses."

CLOSE-UPS AND CONTINUITY

Film people admire professionals. Given a choice between two actors (all else being equal), professionalism will be the deciding factor. Competence is a crucial, basic quality treasured far more than erratic brilliance. It implies an understanding of the extra disciplines that filming demands. You've got to know how to help the camera. In a close-up, the camera lens magnifies your actions, so you have to know how to scale down the action of your performance without losing the intensity as the shot gets tighter. The film actor knows how to reduce a performance physically but not mentally. In fact, oddly enough, your mind should work even *harder* in a close-up than it does during other shots because in the close-up, the performance is all in your eyes; you can't use the rest of your body to express yourself.

The Eyes Have It

When you are the on-camera actor in a close-up, never shift your focus from one eye to the other. Sounds odd, doesn't it? But when you look at something, one of

GET CARTER
Directed by Michael Hodges.   MGM, 1971.

your eyes leads. So during a close-up, be especially careful not to change whichever eye you are leading with. It's an infinitesimal thing, but noticeable on the screen. The camera misses nothing! Another tip from my own experience: when it is my close-up being shot, I pick the off-camera actor's eye that is closest to the camera and look at it with my eye that is furthest from the camera. This turns my face more squarely toward the camera, so as much of my full face as possible is in the shot.

And I don't blink. Blinking makes your character seem weak. Try it yourself: say the same line twice, first blinking and then not blinking. I practiced not blinking to excess when I first made this discovery, went around not blinking all the time and probably disconcerted a lot of people. But by not blinking you will appear strong on screen. Remember: on film that eye can be eight feet across.

I emphasize the eyes because that's where it all happens, especially in a close-up. Don't make faces. What I call "pulling faces" happens when an actor is insecure and starts signaling to the audience. He sends messages, facial twitches, that indicate "This is what you're supposed to feel," or "This is where you're supposed to laugh." An audience picks up on that and will resent it. They don't want to be nudged into a reaction: they want to react spontaneously to what appears to be spontaneous. Just rely on your character's thought processes and your face will behave normally. It's no good practicing in front of a mirror because in the mirror is you—someone you've

THE ITALIAN JOB
Directed by Peter Collinson.   Paramount, 1969.

been seeing all your life—someone who's got nothing to do with who you are in the movie. You are someone else.

The Set-Up

During a take, the camera does not necessarily physically move closer to or away from you, so it's important to ask beforehand what kind of shot is being set up. *Ask* so that you'll know how to gauge the scale of your performance. Here's a rough guide: in the master shot (or long shot) you can afford to be broad; in the medium shot, cut the size of the action to half; and in the close shot, cut the size to half again. Also, you need to know what kind of shot is being set up so you'll know what will be included in the frame. You may be fiddling with your glasses in your lap during a long shot, but if you're still fiddling during the medium shot, when you're not visible below the waist, everyone will say, "What's going on down there below the frame?" You can fling your arms about in a long shot, but not in a close-up, and some directors go in for really massive close-ups. If you think you're in that kind of situation, ask, "How much freedom do I have here?" If the director says you can't move an inch, then you can't move an inch. In the old days you could tell what kind of shot was being set up by the kind of lens on the camera; they used to put a small device on the camera that said "40mm" so you were clued in. Now they've got these great zoom lenses, so I might still be fiddling with my glasses and not know they've changed into a close-up. When in doubt, ask!

The camera doesn't *necessarily* move toward you during a shot; but if they put the camera unusually close, I suggest you get worried—especially if it's a small, hand-held camera. These cameras are very mobile and are, therefore, useful in confined spaces; but if you get too close to them, you move into the curve of the lens. The lens pulls your face back around the curve, so that on the screen you've got a great big nose and your ears go back as though you're riding a motor bike into a strong wind. They used to use lenses like that in topless photography. Unless the director has that effect in mind, I suggest you don't move any closer to the camera at such times.

Off-Camera

Of course, you're not always the center of attention. Sometimes you're the off-camera actor. Then it's important to know how to cooperate in the other actor's close-up, when you'll be feeding him his cues off-camera. Some actors let up on their performances when they are safely out of shot, but that approach doesn't do them any service because it will affect the scene as a whole. Acting is not a competition; everything must be done for the good of the film or else everybody loses—it is not about making yourself seem better than the other guy. When you're the off-camera actor, play with the same intensity as when you are visible. To help the on-camera actor, stand close to the cameraman and get your head as near the lens as possible. This brings the other actor to the most advantageous position for him, which is with his face angled well toward the lens while looking at you. If you were acting with Orson Welles, you could have gone home during his close-up. Orson never wanted anyone in his sight line, never even wanted anyone reading him cues. He did his scenes alone, allowing exactly the right pauses for the other actor's lines. Another actor would have disturbed Orson's concentration. He preferred to imagine that other actor and concentrate on his own bits, rather than be thrown by a less-than-perfect performance. And, in truth, few actors are as good off-camera as on; often they even fluff their lines. Don't be one of those.

ALFIE
Directed by Lewis Gilbert.   Paramount, 1966.
Pictured with Shelley Winters.

Physical Continuity

There is, of course, the continuity person who notes every movement, gesture, and detail of costume that occurs in the master shot, so that all of it can be duplicated in succeeding shots. But it's part of a film actor's job not to confuse the issue. I've already said how important it is to not invent fiddly business that makes it tougher on everybody, and that definitely includes smoking. *Never* smoke in a long shot. When the time comes for the close-up, where did you take that puff? When did you change hands? How long was the ash? Start getting complicated during the master, and the whole scene may go out the window when they come to the close-up. Time and time again you'll hear some actor who is desperate to be creative say, "I'll undo my buttons while he's talking and then I'll do this and then I'll do that." And when it's time for the close-up, the director will say, "Where exactly do you do that?" And the actor will have to say, "I don't know." Then the master will have to be shot again, and the actor will have wasted precious time and money and will definitely have reduced his chances of further employment.

Emotional Continuity

In addition to being aware of visual continuity, the truly professional film actor has to be aware of emotional continuity. In the theatre, a play flows along in sequence, allowing each actor to feel the emotional build and creating the company's sense of the whole. In the cinema the end result may be more realistic, but the process is definitely more artificial. Films are rarely shot in sequence. They are shot in sequence whenever possible, but economics has a way of interfering with that scheme. If the whole unit is on an expensive location, all the location scenes will be shot first, no matter when they come in the script; it's just cheaper that way. If the last scene in a picture takes place outside, you can count on the fact that it

DRESSED TO KILL
Directed by Brian de Palma.   Filmways, 1980.

will get shot first and then you will move to the studio to shoot all the scenes leading up to it. You might shoot the master in the morning, then rush out in the afternoon to shoot another scene because suddenly the sun came out. Then you have to come back some other time and continue with the morning scene, then perhaps do the medium shot and close-up a week later. The director will tell you what he wants in the close-up because that's his job. But it's your job to remember the emotional nature of the master in complete detail. This requires great concentration; you have to summon up a sense memory of the scene in wide shot. If you prepared properly in the first place—that is, married your voice and movement by moving backward while saying your line, then forward to hit the mark—it's all there in your memory, waiting to be summoned. All that initial work is worthwhile because in the close-up, you not only have to repeat what you did in the master, you've got to do it a lot better.

If during the studio scenes, there is a fight sequence and you do it brilliantly but rip your coat, continuity says, "We've got to do the fight again because you don't have a ripped coat in the scene we've already shot." You even worry about cutting your face shaving. For six weeks you can't sit in the sun on your day off because your skin color will change—no sun for you because they're wandering about with Polaroids, comparing you with the previous scene. So you sit still and try not to change.

People say, "Isn't it boring just sitting there for hours?" Well, I don't *just* sit there for hours; I sit there for hours thinking about what I need to do next.

THE ART OF SPONTANEITY

Movie acting is a delicate blend of careful preparation and spontaneity. The art of new-minting thoughts and dialogue comes from listening and reacting as if for the first time. When I was very young and in repertory theatre, I was given some advice by a clever director. He said:

"What are you doing in that scene, Michael?"

"Nothing," I said. "I haven't got anything to say."

"That," said the director, "is a very big mistake. Of course, you have something to say. You've got wonderful things to say. But you sit there and listen, thinking of wonderful things to say, and then *you decide not to say them.* That's what you're doing in that scene."

And that's the greatest advice I can give to someone who wants to act in movies. Listen and react. If you're thinking about your lines, you're not listening. Take your response from the other person's eyes, listen to what he says as though you have never heard it before. Even if you're rehearsing. Actually, rehearsing can be a good test of your spontaneity: if you're running lines with another actor and the assistant director comes up and says, "Sorry to interrupt your rehearsal," you've failed. If he comes up and says, "Sorry to interrupt your chat," then you're on the right course. Your lines should sound like spontaneous conversation, not like acting at all. And that comes from actively listening.

Movie actors earn their living and learn their craft through listening and reacting. I noticed that American actors always try to cut down their dialogue. They say, "I'm not going to say all this. You say that line." At first I couldn't figure out why; I came from theatre, where you covetously count your lines. But it's a smart approach for

© 1982 Warner Bros Inc.

DEATHTRAP
Directed by Sidney Lumet.   Warner Brothers, 1982.
Pictured with Christopher Reeve.

an actor to give up lines in the movies because while you wind up talking about them, they wind up listening and reacting. It's no accident that Rambo hardly speaks. Sylvester Stallone is not a fool. I remember when I first went to America, right after I made *Alfie*. I met John Wayne in the lobby of the Beverly Hills Hotel. He'd just got out of a helicopter, he was dressed as Hondo and he came over and introduced himself to me. I said:

"I do know who you are, Mr. Wayne."

He said, "You just come over?"

"Yeah."

He said, "Let me give you a piece of advice: talk low, talk slow, and don't say much."

When I said I was going to do *Educating Rita*, my friends said:

"*Educating Rita?* That must be about Rita; what are you playing?"

I said, "I'm playing a guy named Frank."

"Well," they said, "you should be doing a picture called *Educating Frank* if you're going to star in a movie."

Everybody thought I was nuts. But I knew that while in the theatre the audience might have looked at Rita because she has so many lines, in the movies the camera has to cut to Frank to get his reactions; otherwise what Rita says has no further meaning. I can't say it enough: one of the most important things an actor can do in a motion picture is to listen and react as freshly as if it were for the first time.

Of course, you needn't stare at people too intently when you're listening to them. In real life, when you listen to people, your eyes go up and down, you look around, you play with your glasses, and then look back at the person. One of the finest practitioners of this technique is Marlon Brando. He *denies* the camera his eyes. Half the time he's looking down or away. Then suddenly he looks up, and you are absolutely fascinated by his eyes.

Freshness becomes a perishable quality after several takes. I'm known as One-Take Mike. That's because I gear myself up to take the risk on "Action!" and it's difficult for me to get the same sense of danger in the very next take. So I usually go off a bit in take two and later I get better again. But I have worked with actors who never get it right the first time but improve with each take. The director has to juggle each actor's different capability to strike the balance that's right for the whole.

Often you may be asked to do a scene again and again, either to get you to the heart of an emotion or to simply exhaust you. The director keeps at you relentlessly until you're totally exhausted. The remarkable thing about exhaustion is that it leads naturally to relaxation. During each take, you change your interpretation by a whisker to keep your performance from getting boring or stale. (I never change physical movements, though, to avoid continuity problems.) It can be bloody annoying when you think you've been great and the director says, "Go again." But the art of the game is to, at least, not get any worse. Most sensible directors, once they've got what they want in the can, say, "Right. We'll print that one. Now we'll just do one for the hell of it. Let yourself go. Have fun, relax." Usually that's the take that's finally used because everyone is so relieved to be free of the responsibility that they give their best performances of all.

© ITC Library Sales.

THE EAGLE HAS LANDED
Directed by John Sturges.   Columbia, 1975.
Pictured with Donald Sutherland and Jean Marsh.

Less is more. That's one of the hottest tips I can give
any young film actor. To do nothing at all can be very
useful in extreme reactive situations. For example, if
something terrible happens to you in the script, like you
find your wife murdered, and they cut to your close-up,
very often you can do a completely blank look. The
audience will project their own emotions on your face.
The acting is in the buildup to that moment, not in the
moment itself. You don't have to do anything, and the

73

audience will go "Blimey!" For the final shot of Greta Garbo in *Queen Christina*, the director told her to remain impassive and the result is an absolute tearjerker. The audience knows what Christina is feeling because the actress has led them through Christina's emotions earlier in the film. At the end, the audience does all the work.

VOICE, SOUND, LIGHTING, MOVEMENT

Voice and Sound

However your voice sounds, use it. It's yours and there's no reason why the character you play shouldn't sound like you. You might need to adopt an accent for a particular character, but that is another subject. Voice consciousness is the pits; it dispels all illusions of reality. If you try to smoothe your voice out—beautify and mellow it—you will no doubt produce a sound like "acting" in the worst old-fashioned sense.

As in theatre, however, learn to produce your voice correctly. Breathe from your diaphragm. If you breathe properly, your voice will be comfortable to listen to because you will not have to strain to get your voice out. Strained speaking makes for strained listening. Some actors speak correctly but their voices are strained or strangulated because they are speaking only from the throat. *Where* the voice comes from is all you have to worry about—really. Breathe from your diaphragm and your nerves won't have a chance to strangle your performance.

On *Zulu* I was incredibly nervous from the start, as you can imagine—my first big movie, my first big chance. The memory of the first day on location still makes me shudder. The uniform was uncomfortable in the boiling hot South African sun. I had to speak in this clipped upper-class accent—an effort, to say the least. Then, to cap it all, my horse threw me into the river three times and I kept having to change my clothes. Finally the damned horse behaved well enough for me to get out my line: "Hot day, hard work." The director, Cy Endfield, shouted:

"CUT! Why is your voice so high?"

I said, "It's the character."

"No!" he said. "I heard you in rehearsal and it was different. It's higher now."

He had the sound technician play my line back. I was so nervous that my throat had tightened, my shoulders became tense, and my voice was about an octave higher than usual. I had to ride that bloody horse across the river again; but this time I *forced* myself to relax, and I got it right.

Stage actors have to calculate when they can take a breath because they need to control the pacing of a speech. But in film, the pacing comes in the editing. The editor can shorten a pause if it goes on too long or lengthen one where it's needed. So in film acting, space your words as the thoughts dictate. Hesitate if the mental process is hesitant; push on if the ideas are flowing fast and fluently. If you are thinking as the character and have made yourself relax, your lungs will instinctively do their work. If they won't, then the character must be having breathing difficulties anyway. Use it; it's naturalism.

Voice projection is necessary in a theatre, where you have to be heard in the last row of the balcony. In the movies, projection isn't usually required. (Pay no attention to the sound technician; he *always* has a problem.) Sensitive microphones can pick up the softest delivery. There may be a boom mike on a pole over your head or you may be wearing a body mike connected to a transmitter. Either way, as the occasion calls for it, you can speak in a barely audible whisper or you can let it rip and be as loud as you want. The sound technician, however, has to know in advance because he's wearing the earphones. I remember I was doing a little sound feature picture in which I played some sort of hoodlum. I had to come up behind a guy and whisper, "You're gonna die," and then shoot him in the back. The sound technician had his equipment turned up high so he could hear the whisper. I forgot to say the line and fired the shot. The sound technician had full volume on his earphones, and the sound of the shot nearly burst his eardrums. He went away and took a lot of aspirin.

Don't get infected by the pace or energy level of another actor's speech. Sometimes underplaying can spread like an epidemic. Keep your own sense of the volume and energy levels you're on. This awareness will also help you to match your previous delivery during a retake because

BULLSEYE!
Directed by Michael Winner. 21st Century Productions, 1990.
Pictured with Sally Kirkland, Roger Moore, and Deborah Barrymore.

unless the director asks you to change your delivery, you have to be able to reproduce it again and again.

Accents

Approach with caution. If you decide to use an accent, you will be bound to expend at least 50 percent of your concentration on that accent, sapping valuable energy that won't be available when the moment most needs it. If you possibly can, play a part in your own manner of speech. That's always preferable to adopting an accent, unless, of course, the accent *is* the performance. In *Treasure Island*, for example, Robert Newton made his manner of speech the entire performance, and it worked.

And about British accents: it's not that Americans don't understand them; the real problem is that we speak twice as fast as Americans do. If you are British and do a picture that is going to be shown in the States, speak slower. I've trained myself to speak very slowly, and Americans accept me, even in an American part. I'm accepted in a Woody Allen picture set in Manhattan because I say "elevator" instead of "lift," "sidewalk" instead of "pavement," "apartment" instead of "flat," and I don't clip along at the British rate of speech. I use their phraseology and I slow down.

It has always annoyed me that people think a Cockney accent is the whole performance. I played three entirely different kinds of Cockney in *Alfie, The Ipcress File,* and *Get Carter*—totally different characters—but everyone said, "Here's his old Cockney performance again." No one says, "Here's Laurence Olivier's old Shakespearean king again." So I played a German in *The Last Valley.* I thought that the obvious trap was to play a German like a man trying to do a German accent; so I decided to play my character like a German trying to speak perfect English. I hired dialect records and listened to them non-stop for a few days. Then I put it out of my mind and tried to speak good English but with a German's basic speech pattern. I think it worked out pretty well.

Another German accent was required for *The Eagle Has Landed*, but this posed an interesting variation. I needed two versions of a German accent. In some scenes, my character was supposed to be speaking German to other Germans, but the script was in English, so any "accent" had to be almost subliminal. Then in other scenes, the character was in England passing himself off as an Englishman, speaking what for him was a foreign language. For that accent, I invented a sort of brusque, clipped sound (which, I hope, was a fairly subtle solution).

Sound and Dubbing

In British films, the sound technician tries to get rid of any extraneous noises on the sound track—for example, the noise of cutlery on a plate. He puts bits of putty under the plates and all that. The Americans just live with the clatter. That's because the British make talking pictures; Americans make moving pictures. We British filmmakers have a theatre tradition, whereas Hollywood was about 3,000 miles away from America's theatre center. In the wide open spaces around California, they first put Westerns on film, while in Europe we started out with Sarah Bernhardt doing bits from the classics. So an American sound technician says, "That's the sound it makes when you put a knife down, so we'll leave it like that." But as an actor, you can help yourself by not putting the knife down just when you say, "I love you, darling." And never shut a door or open a drawer on your own line.

After a film is finished, you may be called in to do some post-synching or dubbing—fitting a new sound (such as a section of your speech) in place of what they've got. Maybe an airplane went over when you said one of

THE SWARM
Directed by Irwin Allen.   AIP/Warner Brothers, 1978.

your lines or maybe the director wants a different inflection. For me, post-synching is a laborious pain in the neck and a great deal of hard work that ends up diminishing my performance in those bits by about 25 percent. Dubbing always happens a long time after you've finished shooting. You've probably done another picture by then. Then, suddenly, you're back in your old character. You see this completely strange person on the screen with funny hair and a moustache, and you think, "God, how did I sound at that time?" I just listen to a bit of it and impersonate myself.

Dubbing is the ultimate control over voice in films, even to the extent sometimes of matchng one actor's voice to another actor's face. One legendary purpose of this phenomenon was to give the producer's mistress a better voice. Sometimes what is called "a scratch track" is recorded on location. It's not of a high technical standard but serves merely as rough guide. You're called back after shooting to dub in your whole part in the controlled environment of a studio. In these circumstances you can sometimes improve on your original delivery a bit. But, generally, post-synching is quite tough. You may have to try several times before you can accurately synchronize sound and image, and it can be difficult to recapture your entire performance. It's harder still if you are dubbing someone else's performance and hardest of all if you didn't like what you did in the first place.

But most directors prefer to record on the set because those extraneous sounds, the ambience, and spontaneous performances have a power of suggestion that you just can't equal by dubbing. Most microphones are much more sensitive than the human ear, and there is a mass of small noises that enrich a sound track that has been made on the set.

Richard Widmark once gave me a piece of advice about large noises in film. He said:

"Watch the special effects when you're working, especially in Westerns."

I said, "Why is that, Dick?"

"What?" he said. "Can you talk into my other ear?"

So I said, "Why is that, Dick?" into his other ear.

He says, "You know all those scenes in pictures where you see the cowboy and he ducks back, and the explosive goes off in the rocks? You talk to any one of us. We're all deaf in one ear."

Henry Fonda, who was also there, joined in then and asked, "What did he say?"

So I said, "You made a lot of Westerns, too, didn't you, Hank?"

"Yeah, I did," he said.

All those fellows really were deaf in one ear. It was the price they paid for being in Westerns.

Lighting and the Inky-Dink

Most stars have a grip on the technical side of

filmmaking because it's in their best interests to know. Making films is a technical process first; any mystery involved comes in with wishful thinking. You need to know what kind of lighting is most flattering to you and most appropriate for each scene; and you must cooperate fully with the lighting technician.

Some stars are very particular about what they want from lighting. One day I was doing the off-camera part for Hank Fonda during his close-ups. I was standing there and we're about to do the scene, and Fonda says, "Where's the inky-dink? Where's the tiny light?" The lighting guy says, "Oh, I forgot, Mr. Fonda. Sorry." And he goes and brings it in. You always wondered about the wonderful way Hank looked in close-ups? He had a gleam in his eyes and a slightly watery, sad look. Well, it was thanks to the inky-dink. Instead of looking at my face, he put this tiny light where my face was and stared straight into that light while I talked behind it.

Movement

Obviously the way you move will be affected by the character you are playing; but natural movement comes from your "center," from the same place as a natural voice. When you walk from your center, you will project a solid perspective of yourself. Walk with that certainty and ease, and your path becomes a center of gravity. Your force pulls all eyes to you. Slouch or poke your head forward, or pull your shoulders back uncomfortably, and that power seeps away. Only a relaxed, centered walk creates a sense of strength. A centered walk can be very menacing, too. Even if you don't get film work on the basis of this advice, follow it and you'll never get mugged, either. Mind you, if you look like I do you'll never get mugged anyway because people generally think I just have been mugged.

One important piece of technical advice about movement: don't rush it. Give the camera operator a chance. James Cagney gave me this tip about running: "When the director tells you to run from over there right toward the camera and past it, run like hell when you're far away, and as you get near the camera, slow down. Otherwise you'll go by so fast, they won't know who the hell went by." Another point: if you're sitting down for a close-up and have to rise, stand up slowly. Don't make any violent movements or you'll pop out of the frame. In other words, always take the camera with you; give the camera operator a chance to crank his wheels and follow you.

Lots of actors study dance or work out to keep themselves ready for any physical challenge. There are also those who know the challenge will never come because of their own physical limitations. But whether you're athletic or not, you should have a heightened sensibility about movement as it relates to character. In this realm, quite small physical manifestations, like nervous hand movements, can be just as effective as a physically demanding pratfall. You don't need to go to a gym to acquire this talent. All you need is sharp-eyed observation of other human beings.

Characters

" When becoming a character,
you have to steal.
Steal whatever you see.
You can even steal from
other actors' characterizations;
but if you do,
only steal from the best."

The moment you pick up a script, you start to make certain deductions about the character you are going to play. It's like picking up clues. The writer gives you some hints and, if you are lucky, you will also have insights based on your experience of life. You may also use your observations of other people who perhaps resemble your character in some way. When I played Frank, the alcoholic university lecturer in *Educating Rita*, I based him on two people I know because while I knew what it was like to be drunk, alcoholism was another thing; and I had no concept of how a university lecturer behaves. (I'd never been to a university.)

So I based Frank-the-lecturer partly on a writer friend of mine named Robert Bolt, who was a great teacher. I knew how he functioned with people—I'd seen him talking and explaining, I knew his manner. And for Frank-the-alcoholic I imagined myself to be another friend of mine named Peter Langan, my partner in a restaurant and someone who behaved like an alcoholic of truly historic proportions. I amalgamated the two people to make Frank. The day that Peter Langan saw the film, he said, "That was based on me, wasn't it?" I said, "Yes."

EDUCATING RITA
Directed by Lewis Gilbert.   Columbia, 1983.
Pictured with Julie Walters.

When becoming a character, you have to steal. Steal whatever you see. You can even steal from other actors' characterizations; but if you do, only steal from the best. If you see Vivien Leigh do something, or Marlon Brando or Robert de Niro or Meryl Streep do something that fits your character, steal it. Because what you're seeing them do, they stole.

The best movie actors become their characters to such an extent that the product isn't viewed by an audience as a performance. It's a strange situation, but in film a person is a person, not an actor; and yet you need an actor to play the person. About twenty years ago, when I was doing *The Ipcress File*, I heard the director, Sid Furie, say, "I need a butcher in this part." Someone suggested that he get a real butcher who knew how to cut up meat authentically. Furie answered: "If I've got a good actor, I've got a real butcher. If I've got a real butcher, the minute I put him in front of the camera he's stiff and I've got a bad actor."

You've got to base your character on reality, not on some actor-ish memory of what reality is because, finally, the actor is in charge of the effect he wants. Woody Allen can play a tragic scene about a brain tumor and make the audience laugh. Another actor can fall on a banana skin and make the audience cry. But the audience mustn't see "an actor," they mustn't see the wheels turning. They must see a real person standing there, somebody just like them.

I remember once I played a drunk in repertory and the director stopped me and said, "You're not playing a drunk! You're playing an *actor* playing a drunk. An actor playing a drunk walks crooked and talks slurry; a real drunk tries to walk straight and speak properly . . . drunks are fighting to stay in control." That was very good advice. And remember that as a drunk, your thought processes and your tongue, for once, are not connected; time lapses before a drunk can get it together. Let yourself struggle. Drunks don't react fast. When I played Frank in *Educating Rita*, I tried to control my head (with which a drunk keeps hitting his chest) because I didn't want Rita to see me drunk. I sat in a way that made me seem a foot shorter because I let my muscles go. Drunks are somehow small and rather pitiful. That Frank is a drunk is tragic, even though he appears at times to be funny.

GENRE

Our lives are not comedies or tragedies or dramas. They are a fascinating mixture, an alchemy, really, of all three. You make a mistake if you pigeonhole a script in any one category because you then seriously limit your character. In a comedy film, "trying to be funny" is certain death. First you have to be a real man or woman. *Then* you slide on the banana skin, and then it will be funny. If you are a comedian sliding on a funny banana peel, nobody will laugh because you're not real. The history of the cinema is littered with great comics who failed on the screen largely because they weren't actors; they coud not be *real* up there. Jack Benny's funny routines never failed in the theatre, but initially, when he did his schtick on the screen, he died. The reason? He was being a funny comedian instead of being a real person to whom something funny happened. If you want to borrow from theatre experience in a film comedy, the best way is in the timing of laughs. In film comedies, theatre actors are especially helped by stage know-how because they have a sense memory of a live audience's laughter. I time the laughs according to how the film crew laughed the first time they heard the scene in rehearsal.

THE SWARM
Directed by Irwin Allen.   AIP/Warner Brothers, 1978.
Pictured with Katharine Ross.

In film, a character is a real person. You have to refrain from turning that real person into a type. Some early film directors like John Ford could get away with characters that became archetypes (the chuckwagon cook who is a drunk, for example); but to do that in the cinema today would risk an audience's disbelief. When you look for qualities to use in building your character, avoid the obvious approach whenever possible. One critic compared *Educating Rita* to *My Fair Lady* because in both cases the girl is changed when her mind and tongue are liberated by a teacher. In *My Fair Lady*, Eliza falls in love with Professor Higgins. It would have been easy to be seduced by the cliché of Rita and Frank falling for each other in *Educating Rita*; but I found none of that in our script. I felt very strongly that although Frank does fall in love with Rita, it's never spoken about and is totally unrequited. If the audience of *Educating Rita* had wanted to search for a prototype, the model might have been the Emil Jannings character in *The Blue Angel*, the sad figure who gets nowhere with the girl. It shouldn't occur to an audience (except maybe to an audience of critics) to look anywhere else for an explanation of a character other than in the film being viewed.

When you are stealing details to build characters on, steal only what was real in the first place, not some dusty stereotype. Since I knew that the Jannings character in *The Blue Angel* had a realistic ingredient for Frank, I stole some of that. I gained 35 pounds and grew a beard because there never should have been the possibility of Rita's being sexually attracted to this fat old drunk. But I suspect nobody noticed my *Blue Angel* steal because Frank wasn't the same as that character any more than he was the same as Professor Higgins. Frank was unique.

LOVE SCENES

Speaking of sexual attraction, love scenes often present special technical problems for actors. There's a lot to cope with there, in addition to characterization. Every-

THE MAN WHO WOULD BE KING
Directed by John Huston.   Allied Artists, 1975.

one wonders what it can be like to make love to a total stranger in front of a camera. Well, it might seem like a good idea to get together and break the ice before the actual shooting, but I think that way lies disaster. You're liable to start the intimacy the night before. Then halfway through the picture, you've split up, aren't talking to each other, and miles of film romance lie before you.

I find the way to deal with love scenes is to be extremely professional about the whole thing: this is a job, this is what the two of us happen to have been asked to do—lie in bed naked—and it doesn't matter that we have never met before. Actually, you're rarely naked, but you do get into some intimate positions and, of course, you do kiss properly. My solution to the potential awkwardness is to joke about it a lot so that the actress I'm with is never under the impression that I'm getting off on it. The moment the director says "Cut!" I make a joke to let the woman know that there was no real passion involved. Such scenes could be embarrassing, but I've done them so often now that there's no sensuality in the process. And then there's the problem for the actress; she has to get herself into a frame of mind where she'd able to let a strange man stroke her bum. But it's all just part of the job, and none of us can afford to be coy about it. But what makes me laugh is that the only time a director ever demonstrates things to you is in the love scenes! Suddenly he feels the need to show you exactly *how* to hold the actress.

There is one practical consideration that makes life more pleasant for everyone under these circumstances: I

By courtesy Dial Trading Ltd.

THE ROMANTIC ENGLISHWOMAN
Directed by Joseph Losey.   Independent, 1975.
Pictured with Kate Nelligan.

always carry mouth spray. I have a quick squirt just before a love scene; the actress says, "What's that?" I say, "Have a taste" and spray her, too. It gets us both over that potential problem.

But despite all manner of professionalism, it can still be somewhat embarrassing to shoot love scenes on a crowded location. It requires fierce concentration to screen out hecklers. In *Alfie*, I had to run out into Notting Hill Gate—an area that is not populated with sensitive drama lovers—and shout, "Darling! Come back! I love you!" The guys on the street started heckling me. The director told me not to worry about the sound because he would post-synch it later. So I struggled with "Come back, come back, I love you," while all this razzing was going on around us. You just have to block it out. The moment you feel foolish, you look foolish. Concentrate, block it out, and relax. Of course, that's not always easy. When I did *Deathtrap*, there was a scene in which I had to kiss Christopher Reeve. He's bigger than I am and, quite honestly, I'd never kissed a man in my life, other than my Dad. Cranking myself up for the task was murderously hard. To an extent, joking still helped: I said to Chris, "If you open your mouth, I'll kill you." I'm afraid Chris and I overcame this problem not with technique or any emotion, but with a bottle of brandy between us.

ROLE MODELS, RESEARCH AND YOU

When you flesh out a character to make him real, your tools are the aspects of yourself that apply, and your role models. People always think the character Alfie was close to my own personality, but while I understood Alfie, I wasn't like him. I based him on a guy named Jim Slater, my best friend when I was young. I could never get any girls, and Jim got them all. He would have been perfect in the part, except that he was always too tired.

I also used Jim as the person to whom I was talking when I had to speak directly to the camera. Normally when you look directly into the lens, the effect will be very phoney because the filmmaker is breaking the illusion of eavesdropping on reality. But in *Alfie*, my

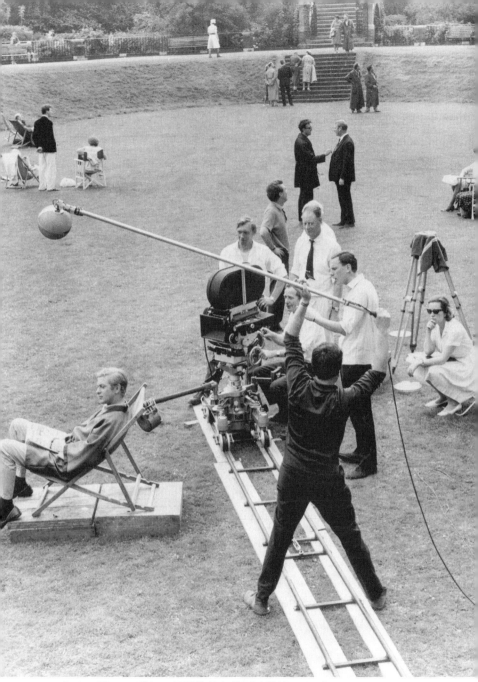

ALFIE
Directed by Michael Gilbert.   Paramount, 1966.
On location.

character spoke to the audience through the camera, a bit like the technique of "asides" in the theatre when a character detaches himself from the action and addresses the audience directly. In fact, when I first spoke directly to the camera, I treated it like a large audience. The director, Gilbert Lewis, said, "Cut! Come closer to the camera. Do it as if you were talking to just one person, so that every member of the audience feels as if you're singling him out personally." Then I played the moment as though I were talking to Jim. We liked each other, and Jim was really interested in what I had to say. He would have especially appreciated remarks like, "She's in beautiful condition," when Alfie was running his hands over a woman's bum, because Jim used to say things like that. That confidence in Jim's appreciation is what won me the collusion of the cinema audience, even when they didn't really approve of Alfie's goings-on.

Sometimes you have to play a character with whom you have absolutely nothing in common. In *The Romantic Englishwoman*, I was cast completely against type, as the sort of man I would despise if I met him in real life. He was totally unable to take effective action. Now I'm not completely an action man, but at worst I'm a catalyst; this character I was playing just let his life go wrong all around him without doing anything about it. He was a rich novelist who lived in the plush stockbroker belt, mixed with pseudo-intellectuals, and did absolutely nothing to stop his wife from going off on a romantic adventure. The character was completely non-chemical; everything about the part was against my nature.

But once you have reached that kind of conclusion about a character, you have to put it out of your mind. In real life, each person is always in sympathy with his own motives; and I had to find the reasons for this man's behavior. I ended by thoroughly enjoying the part because I submerged my own personality entirely and invented everything: if I would have gone north, I made this character go south; if some piece of behavior was alien to me, I figured it was probably right for him.

In historical pictures, research can sometimes be a valuable guide in finding what's real for a character. Often we have stereotyped views of how people behaved in other periods and places, and research often disproves a stereotype and makes life more interesting for the actor. For example, in *Zulu* I was cast as a wishy-washy upper-crust Victorian officer. Now, I wasn't in a very strong position to make radical suggestions about interpretation. I had got the part by the skin of my teeth. Originally I'd gone to audition for the part of a Cockney private, but they'd already cast that role. However, since I was tall and fair, I apparently looked like a posh Englishman, and the director, Cy Endfield, asked if I could do an upper-class accent. I switched quickly to Etonian and said, "Why, Mr. Endfield, I've been doing it for years." He had me do a screen test, during which I showed my absolute terror. He came up to me at a party the following night, after ignoring me most of the evening, and said, "That was the worst damn screen test I ever saw in my life." I thought, okay, so I haven't got it. "But," he continued, "you've got the part because we're

BLAME IT ON RIO
Directed by Stanley Donen.   20th Century-Fox, 1983.
Pictured with Michelle Johnson.

leaving on Monday and we can't find anybody else."

Cy Endfield and Stanley Baker (who was the producer and also the star) both saw my character, Lieutenant Gonville Bromhead, as a chinless wonder who treated war as though it were a game on the playing fields of Eton. Stanley wanted the character played like a weedy Hooray Henry what-ho type, as a contrast to the character he was playing. But I had found a history book in a secondhand bookshop in Charing Cross Road with a photograph of the real Lieutenant Bromhead. He was 5"6' tall, had a black beard, and in no way corresponded to this vacillating upper-class twit they were envisaging. I showed the picture to Baker, saying, "Listen, Stan, I know your character has to overpower my character in the end because that's the story. But wouldn't it be better to overpower a man who is strong and believes in himself, rather than the kind of fellow who says 'Hullo, chaps, and all that'? The kind of fellow everyone knows immediately Stanley Baker could make mincemeat of? There's no clash of personality unless my character has some strength."

Baker and Endfield thought it over and agreed with me. So I was allowed to play Lieutenant Bromhead as something quite different than the way he was written. And that part was my first big break. If nothing else, we put the record straight about the stereotyped view of Victorian officers as upper-class caricatures.

The Man Who Would Be King, which was adapted from a story written in 1888 by Rudyard Kipling, was another film in which background knowledge proved indispensable. The director, John Huston, had been trying to get this film off the ground for years. In fact, it was a bit daunting to learn that he had originally wanted to cast

Clark Gable and Humphrey Bogart in the parts that Sean
Connery and I played. I was cast as Peachy and Sean
played Danny: we were a couple of rogues, formerly
sergeants in the army of Queen Victoria, now gun-
runners in India planning to set ourselves up as kings in a
remote Himalayan stronghold.

We all spent days talking about the script before we
even shot a foot because Huston wanted us to achieve a
Victorian view of society. For example, Peachy had to
throw an Indian off of a moving train, for no real reason.
From a contemporary perspective, that seems inexplicable
and barbaric. But from the standpoint of Victorian values,
this high-handed attitude toward the natives was the
norm. Furthermore, Peachy and Danny had experienced
their own humiliations at home as members of the
working class at a time when class divisions in England
were as tough as apartheid is now in South Africa. So
when I tossed that Indian off the train, I had to bear in
mind that Peachy might well have been tossed off a train
by a member of the English aristocracy.

Everyone kept telling Sean and me that we were
making another *Butch Cassidy and the Sundance Kid*. We
weren't. It's no good getting into the imitation game; all
you get is a pale copy. But Sean and I did come to the
conclusion pretty quickly that we had to be a double act,
and a generous double act. We had to give each other
complete collaboration for the sake of the picture. We
had a choice: we could edge each other out and get
individual close-ups, or we could bring each other into

close-up for the most interesting lines and improve the film as a whole. This was the best relationship I've ever had with another actor; we gave to each other all the time. It made it much easier to become those characters.

But the great John Huston also helped enormously. He managed to consolidate my character for me in just one sentence. I'd been shooting for about two days and Huston said, "Cut! Michael," he said, "speak faster; he's an honest man." Because I was speaking slowly, it seemed as though I was trying to figure out what effect I was making. Huston's observation was spot on. Honest men speak fast because they don't need time to calculate.

After three days of shooting, Huston wasn't calling Sean and me by our own names anymore; he was calling us Danny and Peachy. Sean and I got to the point where not only *could* we improvise some of the dialogue, but this director, who for twenty-six years had nurtured this script that he co-authored, actually *let* us improvise the dialogue.

BILLION DOLLAR BRAIN
Directed by Ken Russell.   United Artists, 1967.

Behavior On and Off the Set

"No matter what the reason,
if you start to scream and shout,
you look a fool,
and you feel a fool,
and you earn the
disrespect of everyone."

THE UPSTAGER, THE SCENE-STEALER, AND THE STALLER

Almost without exception, actors help each other. In the movie business, the list of people whose careers suddenly ground to a halt is the same as the list of actors who tried to make enemies or pull tricks. That kind of behavior doesn't usually work anyway because the guv'nor—the director—is watching. He knows what's phoney and who's trying to screw up somebody else. He'll see it and he'll put a stop to it. And if tricks get past a director, an audience will sense them subliminally; they may not understand how a piece of acting skullduggery is achieved, but they have instinct and they'll say, "I didn't like that actor." The sort of dirty tricks such actors employ are fairly transparent, really. As in theatre, there is the Upstager: he keeps moving backward a few steps so that the other actors have to turn their backs to the camera to relate to him. Then there's the Scene-Stealer: he's the chap who will put in a little move of the hands or turn of the head during your tense moment and steal focus. The Staller does a slightly more subtle maneuver: he slows down the tempo that was set at rehearsal,

A BRIDGE TOO FAR
Directed by Richard Attenborough.　United Artists, 1977.

extends pauses, talks more hesitantly and generally prolongs the time that the camera is on him, thereby hogging the scene. Few actors actually stoop to all this, and directors usually won't tolerate it. But occasionally only the other actor will notice a trick, and I recommend that you fight back with the same weapons; that usually works like a charm.

TEMPERAMENTS

You won't gain much leverage in the long run by pandering to other people's moods. If you put yourself in the position of yielding to temperaments, you deserve everything you get. During the filming of *The Magus*, I had a confrontation not so much with Anthony Quinn as with Quinn's kowtowers. Every day we'd get a bulletin from one of his minions: "Tony's in a great mood today"; or "Watch out, Tony's in a terrible mood today." One day I said:

"Has he ever asked what mood I'm in?"

The minion said, "Why should he?"

"If you have to ask," I said, "I might as well get the next plane home." And I set off for the airport. They persuaded me to come back, but I'd made my point.

I'm completely against interfering in other people's performances. Get on with your own contribution and leave everybody else to the director. He may be looking for qualities you never thought of, or he may edit the scene in a way you never imagined. And no matter what the other actors do—stop, blow their lines—you continue

SLEUTH
Directed by Joseph L. Mankiewicz.   20th Century-Fox, 1972.
Pictured with Laurence Olivier.

your scene right to the end or until the guv'nor says
"Cut."

INSURANCE

Insurance may sound like a mundane topic. What's it
got to do with movie acting? Well, on a set, the
continuity person writes down everything that happens,

including the cause of a delay on a take—for example, "it rained" or "the door fell off its hinges." The continuity person also writes "Actor, _____, one hour late," if that's the case. If a movie overruns and the budget is blown to bits, the producer goes to his insurance company, and the insurance company asks to see the continuity sheets. If your name features heavily on those sheets, you suddenly find you're not getting the job offers. It doesn't matter how big a star you are; the history of the cinema is littered with people who were uninsurable. Orson Welles, one of the greatest talents in the cinema, couldn't bring in a film on time, and as a result he had great trouble raising money.

STUNTS

Films often make huge physical demands on an actor; but the actor who tells you he does all his own stunts is a bloody liar. Insurance companies almost always prevent actors from doing their own stunt work. When you hit your head, the insurance agent gets the headache.

But, of course, for some pictures, for authenticity, you will have to acquire certain skills, some of which may give you very little pleasure. Actors who can't ride nevertheless must look good on a horse, at least while the camera is rolling. They may, though, fall off five seconds after "Cut!" I had to learn to scuba dive for *Beyond the Poseidon Adventure*. I never thought I could because I'm claustrophobic. But I managed. And there was always a professional diver close by, just in case. If I raised my hand, he would whisk me to the surface—it was like asking to be excused to go to the lavatory.

The vital thing is to know where to draw the line. If necessary, you can say no. After all, you're your own commodity. Your body and your face are all you have to offer, so you need to look after them. On *Billion Dollar Brain*, which was on location in Finland, the director, Ken Russell, wanted me to jump into a hole in the ice. I had a Finnish stand-in, so I went up to him and said:

"Want to earn some extra money? Warm up in the sauna and then jump into that hole in the ice."

He looked at me. "What?"

I said, "You know. Like the Finns do."

He said, "No they don't; they'd have heart attacks."

So he refused to do it, too.

In *The Island* I held up filming for hours, refusing to go into the water because there was a shark. The director, Michael Ritchie, asked me when was the last time I heard of a movie star being eaten by a shark. I said, "I'm not worried about the last time; I'm worried about the first time. I'm not about to be the first movie star to be eaten by a shark."

The only time you will be asked to do a real stunt (which is precisely when you must never do it) is on the last day of shooting, when they don't give a damn what happens to you. Anyway, if you think about it, what's the point of getting an actor to do a stunt when there's a guy

DIRTY ROTTEN SCOUNDRELS
Directed by Frank Oz.   Orion, 1988.

on the set who has trained all his life to do this job? It's selfish to do a stuntman out of his opportunity. So, remember, if an actor tells you he does his own stunts, he's a liar, or selfish, or both.

But one day you're going to be in a studio and the special effects technician is going to come up to you and say something like this:

"On 'Action,' that wall will be blown out, but don't worry about it; it will crash away from you. The roof will come down, but don't worry about it; it won't fall on you. The floor will open up and you'll drop down into some water, and there's a shark, but don't worry; we've taken his teeth out. Then, as you get out of the water, a poisonous snake will crawl up your trousers, but don't worry about it; we've got an expert from the zoo and he's just milked it."

And what you say to him is, "Mr. Special Effects Man, let me see you do it first."

He will say, "We haven't got the time. I'd gladly do it, you know, but we'd have to reset the charge, get the snake out of my trouser leg, put the roof back . . . It would cost fifteen thousand dollars in lost time to do all that; it would take all afternoon to reset. Otherwise I'd do it."

You look at him and you say: "You do it first."

Always have a stunt demonstrated to you before you do it.

PROFESSIONALISM

As a leading actor in the movies, you are paid to pick up a picture on the first day of shooting, put it on your shoulders, and take it triumphantly to the end. But this doesn't give you any right to be a prima donna. I was on a film with another big male star, and because they mucked him about one day and kept him waiting around, when we got on the set the following morning at half past eight, he sent a message saying, "Because you kept me waiting four hours yesterday, I'm going to be four hours late today." We couldn't work without him, so we all just sat there. Everyone was watching me because I was the other co-star; they were wondering how I was going to react when he finally appeared. So when he turns up, I call him over. I say, "Come here." He's looking a bit truculent because he's expecting trouble from me. I say, "Thank God you did that. I was out all night last night, so I was really tired, and I hadn't learned the dialogue. I didn't know this bloody scene. Now I've had three hours sleep, I've learned the dialogue, and everything's fantastic. The point is, I'm going to a party tonight; can you do this again tomorrow?" He was never late again.

I used to lose my temper. I would fly off the handle quite quickly in a work situation. Then I worked on a picture called *The Last Valley* by James Clavell, who had been a prisoner of the Japanese during World War II. James looks like an Englishman, but he really thinks like a Japanese. I lost my temper one day, and James just looked at me and let me finish my ranting and raving. Then he said, "Come with me, Mike. Let's go 'round the corner

DEATHTRAP
Directed by Sidney Lumet.   Warner Brothers, 1982.

and sit down." He sat me down and talked to me about the Japanese theory of losing face. No matter what the reason, if you start to scream and shout, you look a fool, and you feel a fool, and you earn the disrespect of everyone (even if it's the producer you're screaming at). I've never lost my temper in a work situation again. And never, ever, under any circumstances, shout at anybody who is lower on the ladder than you are. It would be taking a monstrously unfair advantage.

KEEPING THE RUSHES IN FOCUS

At the end of each day, people on a film sometimes go to see the rushes. I never do. Everybody buys their yachts after the rushes and goes bankrupt at the premiere. Anyone you speak to about the rushes says they're wonderful. You say to makeup, "How were the rushes?"; and they say, "Just wonderful. Her lipstick was wonderful." You say to hairdressing, "How were the rushes?"; and they say, "Wonderful. You should have seen your wig. It was great." Everybody only watches out for his own thing. If you go to the rushes, you will only watch yourself. But in actual fact, your character should be a stranger to you because it *is* someone else. The director, if he's any good, will tell you what you were like far more accurately than the rushes will. To my mind, all you can tell from rushes is whether you are in focus, and even then the projectionist may have screwed up. You should remember also that if you don't go to rushes, you get home earlier. I'm also known as Quick-Start Mike because the moment I hear "Cut! Wrap!" I'm off and away.

Here's one last tip with a moral for film actors. It's something I noticed after going to Hollywood parties with big-name actors, big-name producers. Every time I went to an actor's house, the walls were covered with pictures of himself. Every time I went to a producer's house, the walls were covered with Lautrecs, Van Goghs, and Picassos. Just bear that in mind.

Directors

"You've got to be flexible.
Directors do a massive amount of
planning and homework,
and if after all that your director
decides to throw it all
out of the window
and shoot spontaneously,
then you must follow his lead."

The director's word is basically law. That's why they say film is "a director's medium." And there are some actors who can take direction, and some who can't. The ones who succeed listen to the director and immediately translate what he says into their performances. They take his direction straight into their bloodstreams. Sometimes a director will hang in there with you, nursing you through every moment of a take. That's an actor's director. Others don't relate to actors at all; they almost dare you to give a good performance. In either case, don't expect any praise. If a director is satisfied with your work, he'll move on to the next shot; if not, he won't. That's the only signal you get. Joe Mankiewicz is bloody marvelous in that respect. He knows what you should want, he knows what you've got, and he also knows when you've got it. He's one of those directors who says nothing if he likes what he sees; but if he starts questioning you, watch out—you know you haven't got it. If he says anything, such as, "Why did you point to her on that line?" you're in trouble. Lucky trouble because he's spotted something in the gesture that's not quite real. Mankiewicz is with you until you're back on track. Don't rest. Don't fight it.

Your craft has to be malleable enough to be shaped and shaped and shaped until the final take.

But not all directors are Joe Mankiewicz. There are good directors and bad directors; you learn something from both. From a bad director you can learn the art of self-preservation—how to give and sustain a performance all from within. And this art, like most arts, is based on craft—the craft of being a real pro. Your self-reliance is just part of being a professional. For better or for worse, until the limo stops picking you up in the morning, you're married to that director. Either you learn to love him, or you fake it. If, however, as occasionally will happen, you've wound up with a complete dummy, you all walk back to the dressing room and say, "Let's do this ourselves." It happened to me in one picture (which I won't mention by name). The director was in the outer reaches of space—and it was clear he'd only bought a one way ticket. I think he might also have been partial to certain substances. Well, we read his altitude early on and quietly agreed to take care of ourselves. And he was credited with having directed a terrific film. On the other hand, I once worked with a director who was a complete and total alcoholic and perfectly competent at the same time. He was bombed all day, and none of us noticed it. Until he fell down a ditch. But these extremes are very rare since once the insurance people slip that little character trait into your dossier, you've had it. They don't write, "Great fun at parties," either. You're out. And "out" doesn't mean "around here" or "statewide." Out means worldwide. The insurance people in the film biz

THE MAN WHO WOULD BE KING
Directed by John Huston.   Allied Artists, 1975.
Pictured with Sean Connery.

live in the global village; you're never out of sight.

Naturally there will be times when actor and director are going to disagree. I compromise. I say, "Okay, we'll do it your way, but could we try it my way as well, and will you look at it in rushes?" An actor never gets to choose which take will finally be used, but he can ask for his choice to be printed so that you can all look at it. The director customarily says, "Yeah, sure, great idea," then usually forgets all about it. But if he doesn't forget, and it goes to rushes, chances are you'll find the director was right. You really can't judge yourself as clearly as the director can; his perception will usually prove sounder than your instinct. Anyway, he's the boss, and you might as well trust him. Some actors can't give in, can't compromise. Big rows take place. If you're a young actor or new to films, I suggest you let the director direct and get on with your job: following his direction.

Different directors call rehearsals for different reasons. Some arrange rehearsals for the benefit of the camera work, for shots that are technically difficult. Some actually call rehearsals for the actors! One director will rehearse a film for two weeks before you start shooting. Another director rehearses one scene and then—bam!—does the take. It's over.

Woody Allen just puts it all on film right from the start, so that the rehearsal and the take become indistinguishable. He just keeps shooting and shooting it. He never covers in close-up. It's all one long shot. It goes on forever. In *Hannah and Her Sisters*, some of the takes involved 360 degrees of shooting all around the house—and not a soundstage set either; a real New York City apartment, a real house. We'd go in at 8:30 in the morning, block out the moves, and shoot at 8:00 at night because it took so long to light. Woody rehearses everything down to the tiniest detail; his camera becomes a microscope. His pictures may look as if they are ad-libbed, but they are brought to that point by solid rehearsal, rehearsal, rehearsal. On camera the flow of the work from a sense of rehearsal—without the pitch of a take—makes for very relaxed and imaginatively disposed actors. Other directors will break it all up. Like John Huston. He'd cut in the middle of a master because he knew in his mind where he wanted the close-up—he didn't need to cover himself by shooting a master all the way through. A less experienced director would want all that footage to cover himself in case he changed his mind later during the editing, but Huston was a master of his craft. His mind was probably made up before the shooting began.

Brian de Palma has a bit of a chilly personality, but I admire him as a director and technician. So when he offered me a rathar weird horror film called *Dressed to Kill*, I figured this was a gamble that might pay off. He was very demanding, often shooting on and on until he got precisely what he wanted. I remember one nine-page sequence that incorporated a 360-degree swing of the camera and required 26 takes (a record for me); whenever we actors got the scene right, the camera didn't and vice versa. That one sequence took a whole day to shoot.

Sometimes a director will insist on a lot of takes for reasons that have little to do with perfecting craft. There's a famous story that Jack Hawkins tells about the filming of *Ben Hur*. He and Stephen Boyd were playing a scene, and the director, Willie Wyler, kept saying:

"No, do it again."

The actors said, "What should we do differently?"

Wyler would say, "I don't know. Just do it again."

Two days later, when they were on take 150, Wyler finally said:

"Print it."

Jack blew his top. "That's the same way we've been doing it for the last hundred takes!" he said.

And Wyler said, "I know, but the next set wasn't ready yet."

Some directors are famous bullies. But a bully needs a victim, and you have to make it clear that you're not the victim type. Before I started work on *Hurry Sundown*, I knew Otto Preminger's reputation for picking on people. So the moment I met him I said:

"You mustn't shout at me."

Taken aback, he said, "Why do you think I would?"

Calmly, I said, "Friends of mine worked with you on *Saint Joan*, and they said you shouted."

He said, "You shouldn't make friends with bad actors. I only shout at bad actors."

He never shouted at me because I'd raised the issue straight away. And I did learn from him how to do a long take in a movie—seven minutes long.

HANNAH AND HER SISTERS
Directed by Woody Allen. Orion, 1985.
Academy Award—Michael Caine—Best Supporting Actor
Pictured with Mia Farrow.

Don't think there aren't gentle directors, though. Carol Reed carried tact so far that in order to save an actor's ego he'd disguise the reason he said, "Cut." Carol always carried a nail or coin in his hand, and when he had to stop a scene because it wasn't going well or because the actor had blown his lines, Carol would drop the nail on the floor and say, "Cut. We must have quiet, you know. Now, since we've stopped anyway, would you mind doing it again?"

Some directors will ask you to improvise during a take, an impromptu approach that can strike panic into performers who are afraid of the slightest alteration from the working plan, the merest departure from the script. But script changes are routinely made at the last minute simply because the writer just hasn't allowed for the physical reality of the shoot. You've got to be flexible. Directors do a massive amount of planning and homework, and if after all that your director decides to throw it all out of the window and shoot spontaneously, then you must follow his lead. You aren't working on an assembly line. A stage set is more like a trampoline. Even with John Huston's meticulously prepared script of *The Man Who Would Be King*, we were expected to improvise. I remember one scene where I was drilling recruits. Now these were all Arabs who didn't understand a word of English. So I really drilled them, making it all up as I went along. There was one spectacular incompetent in the front row, which gave me the opportunity for a very funny scene. It couldn't have happened if I had been told to stick to the script.

Movie scripts are not Holy Writ. As if to prove its fallibility, the director, on the first day on the set of *The Ipcress File*, put the script on the floor, set fire to it, and said, "That's what I think of that." We all stood there looking at each other. I was a bit baffled. "What are we going to shoot?" I said. In the end, the director used my copy. But I was allowed to improvise a lot. My favorite scene was a sequence in which I was shopping in the supermarket while talking to the "M" character, the secret service boss. The director tossed us a few guidelines and off we went—three minutes of ad-libbed dialogue.

BEYOND THE POSEIDON ADVENTURE
Directed by Irwin Allen.   Warner Brothers, 1979.
Pictured with Karl Malden.

————————————

Sometimes you wind up initiating changes yourself, without the director's urging. In *A Bridge Too Far*, I had the luck to be standing next to the man I was actually playing, Lieutenant Colonel Joe Vandeleur, just before I had to order a column of tanks and armored cars into battle. I had always thought that my scripted line, "Forward, go, charge," didn't have an authentic ring, so I asked him what he actually said on the day of the battle. He said, "I just said quietly into the microphone, 'Well, get a move on, then.'" And that's the line I spoke. I felt much more secure as the actor knowing that the character's line had been tested in battle.

Improvisation can work extremely well if the atmosphere is relaxed and you are in tune with your character. Of course, you shouldn't get creative with the script unless you know you can really improve on what's already there on the page. I did a picture called *California Suite*, which was written by the great American comedy writer Neil Simon. He visited the set the first day, came over to Maggie Smith and me and said, "Listen, if you think of anything funny, you know, ad libs, put 'em in. But tell me what they are first. And they better be funnier than what I've written." We thought and we thought. Our poetic license hung heavy on our conscience. And needless to say, we never ad-libbed a word.

Even if the director doesn't edit the film himself, he certainly has the final say over the final cut. The editing can alter the pacing and rhythms of performance—in fact that's what it's for. It not only orchestrates line delivery, it determines how you are emphasized; whether you are in close-up or part of a group. Editing can shape a lot of your performance, and a career can be made or lost by editing. The worst fate, of course, is to be cut out altogether, unless your performance was so bad you're lucky no one will ever see it. Yet even a very good performance may have to go if it adds superfluous elements to a film where they're looking for time cuts. On the other hand, a mediocre performance can be given a shot in the arm by skilled editing—the pacing can be finessed and clumsy moments can be contracted or eliminated. Cutting away to a strong reaction shot on your slightly misplayed line can give the impression that you delivered it far more effectively than you actually did.

I feel about editors the way I do about directors: they know their jobs. You and I are betting that their decisions are right for the film as a whole and that ultimately what's good for the movie is good for us. Recently I dubbed a film called *Without a Clue* and had the chance to see the edited version. There had been a sword fight in the picture, and when I saw the fight on the screen, I said, "You've cut out the funniest moment in the whole film—a slow reaction I did during the fight." The editor said, "I know. You're right. It would have been the funniest moment in the film, but that reaction took five seconds. The scene is at the end of the film, when all the momentum should be gathering. We can't afford to take that much time out of the action however wonderful that isolated moment is. You can't slow things down at the end of a comedy." He ran the sword fight back to show

CALIFORNIA SUITE
Directed by Herbert Ross.   Columbia, 1978.
Pictured with Maggie Smith.

me where my reaction would have been, and he was right. I was sorry to lose that moment, but clearly it had to go. Editors know their business and, honestly, I've never once thought, "Well, if they'd left that moment in the film, I'd have got an Oscar."

But regardless of how good the editing is, no one relies on the editing room to get them out of trouble. Directors want to get it right on the floor. There's a story about George Cukor, who was relentless about getting it right, and Jack Lemmon. Jack had come to Hollywood from the Broadway theatre and George was directing him in his first film role. Jack kept doing a scene, and George kept saying, "Cut. Less, Jack, less." And Jack would do it again.

George: "Cut. Less, Jack, less."

And Jack would do it again.

George: "Cut. Less, Jack, less."

Jack finally said, "If I do any less, I'll be doing nothing."

George: "*Now* you've got it!"

THE MAGUS
Directed by Guy Green.   20th Century-Fox, 1968.
Pictured with Candice Bergen.

On
Being
A
Star

"To be a movie star,
you have to invent yourself."

Movie stardom is not necessary. From my own experience, not a lot of it is recommended. But to be a good movie actor is quite a trip, and one I highly recommend that you take.

I try to remember what it was like to be the new boy. I was on a picture once as a one-day actor; the director was explaining what he wanted me to do, when the star, who definitely was short, walked over to us. He came over, looked me in my chest, and said: "You're fired, kid." "What?" said the director. The actor said, "He's fired. Go and collect your money, kid, and go home." He wasn't about to have anyone in the film taller than he. That old star power still exists and, unfortunately, can still be abused.

To be a movie star, you have to invent yourself. I was a Cockney boy and obviously didn't fit anybody's idea of what an actor was supposed to be, so I decided to put together elements that added up to a memorable package. I got myself seen around the "in" spots, wearing glasses and smoking a cigar. I became known as "that guy who wears glasses and smokes a cigar." Then people began to say, "He plays working-class parts." Suddenly I was "that working-class actor who wears glasses and smokes a cigar." Then word spread that I was quite amenable, so I became "that easy-to-work-with working-class actor who wears glasses and smokes a cigar." It was the truth, but I had quite consciously assembled that truth so nobody could miss it. I did for myself what the major studios used to do for their contract actors. I created an image. Image can be true, false, or in between, but until you have one, for the world of the movies you don't exist.

In fact, I tried to conduct my whole career the way the big studios used to handle their actors. I did as many films a year as I could, to get the experience. If you sit around waiting for "the big one," when that opportunity finally comes along, you won't be ready for it. You won't have all that small time experience that adds up to big time ability. Success, it may surprise some to hear, comes from doing, not negotiating, not counting lines, not weighing credits. Do it, do it, don't wait for it. Some very good actors sit out their entire lives while waiting for the right part. Make every part the one you've been waiting for. Learn the confidence you can only gain under fire. The confidence lends relaxation. Relaxation opens all your resources for the demands of your role. And when the big role does come along you'll need all 100 percent of what you've got to give. Don't be caught 25 percent short; don't be caught one percent short. Be completely available to whatever challenge comes your way, by being

THE ISLAND
Directed by Michael Ritchie.   Universal, 1980.

totally in charge of your craft, your material, yourself.

A star has certain obligations. The money for a film is often raised on his name and the expectation of his continuing and reliable presence. Any scene he's in, he's going to be responsible for. This does not mean that he wants to hog his scene. People have come up to me on a set and said, "Did you see that character actor steal that scene off you yesterday?" And I'll say, "Thank God for that. At least that's five minutes I'm not responsible for."

Obligations continue off the set, too, with interviews, public appearances, promotions. I do all that because it's part of the job. Acting means communication. If no one knows the picture is being released, you've failed to communicate. So the same standards of reliability, good humor, and punctuality are required for the off-the-set duties. Fan mail is important, too (and you can usually write off the expenses). I don't personally answer every letter because that would be impossible. But I do sign every photograph—I don't have a secretary who fakes my signature. Now there are some stars who refuse, temperamentally, to do any off-the-set promoting, but the only actors who get away with that get so much publicity for *not* cooperating that the production company is probably just as happy that they won't.

Temperament usually comes from insecurity. Real stars aren't insecure. They say what they want, and they usually get it. I call the temperamental ones "almost" people: they can almost act, they almost know their lines, they are almost on time, they are almost stars.

Half my energies as a leading man in a picture go into keeping the tensions down. You set the tone on the set.

And when you're the leading man, you're always the one who gets sent to get the leading lady out of the dressing room if she won't come. Everyone says, "I can't get her out—Michael, you go and get her out." She's probably still in there because her hair's not right, or she's not too keen on the director. Very few leading ladies have to get the leading man out of the dressing room.

I always try to have a good relationship with my leading lady. But that's it. You must never get emotionally involved with her. It weakens you, and it weakens the movie. If you're going to be a film star you have to be made of a certain kind of steel.

I choose a script because the part is good for me and because it's different from the last role I did. I look for an acting challenge. But as I get older, I'm also a lot more interested in the circumstances under which a film will be shot. Will it be a little shoestring picture that will have us sitting in mud huts in Tanzania? Or are we going to be put up in the George V in Paris? I never used to look at that side of making a film. I once spent twenty-six weeks in a Philippine jungle which, looking back, could just as well have been the tropical garden at Kew, for all the difference it made to the picture. In the jungle, you can't see the sky, you can't see the scenery. All you can see is jungle. We lived for twenty-six weeks in an unfinished brothel. The rooms were expected to be used for twenty minutes at a time and were furnished accordingly. Twenty-six weeks in rooms like that. And there wasn't a girl in any of them. After that experience, I did *The Magus*

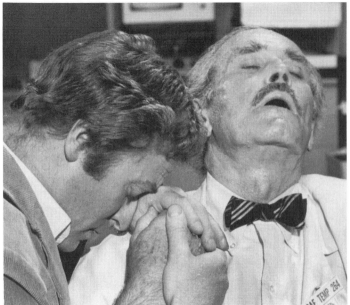

THE SWARM
Directed by Irwin Allen.   AIP/Warner Brothers, 1978.
Pictured with Henry Fonda.

without ever reading the script because the weather in England is lousy in January and I'd get a few weeks in the South of France out it. That choice was a bit of a mistake on some grounds, but in terms of climate, I had a winner. I close a script quickly if it starts, "Alaska: our hero is stumbling through a blizzard . . . "

It's much harder to act in a bad film than in a good one. A terrible script makes for very difficult acting. Yet you can win an Academy Award for some of the easiest acting of your career, made possible by a brilliant script.

There ought to be an award for triumphing over the odds. But nothing is dead certain; you are always taking a risk. On the face of it, *Sleuth* (formerly a very successful play), starring Laurence Olivier and myself, looked promising; but it was a two-handed picture, and no film with just two actors had ever made money—that is, until *Sleuth* was released.

When I analyze myself as a screen actor, I think part of my appeal is that I am not an obvious winner. Put Sean Connery or Charles Bronson up there and you know they are going to win. But I have the air of a loser and I've often played losers in pictures. I spent a large part of my life being a loser, which I think adds an interesting dimension to my personality. It's important to understand what you convey. And you mustn't overlook or ignore the changes that occur. I was sent a script when I was on the cusp of middle age and I sent it back, saying the part wasn't big enough. They rang me up and said, "We don't want you to play the romantic juvenile; we were thinking of you as the father." Actually I enjoy getting older. It's much easier for actors than actresses. All the best roles for an actor of my type are the mature ones. I'm growing up and the roles are growing up with me, like they did for George C. Scott and Lee Marvin. So my middle years are turning out to be my best because I'm getting meatier parts. I'm quite glad to have got through the other lot.

Hollywood is divided up socially into the A Team, the B Team, the C Team, and the Fun Team. The A Team is just a handful: Redford, Eastwood, Stallone, and a few

BULLSEYE!
Directed by Michael Winner.   21st Century Productions, 1990.
Pictured with Roger Moore.

studio heads. I don't belong in there. Those people don't mix with the B Team or the C Team for the simple reason that they don't want to be asked for jobs. But they do mix with the Fun Team. I'm in the Fun Team. I get invited to dinner because I'm reasonably amusing, I have an exceptionally beautiful and intelligent wife, and I have the sense not to ask for jobs. But if I was in the B Team, which I would be if I weren't in the Fun Team, I wouldn't be invited.

Other stars can be useful funds of advice. Peter Finch told me it took him thirty years to find out that you mustn't listen to anybody's opinion at lunch. I endorse that. Eddy Robinson, who was a close friend of mine, used to advise me to buy paintings. When he died, his collection was worth millions. And Peter O'Toole told me not to play small parts, even in vehicles that would get a lot of exposure, because that would make me a small-part actor. He advised me to play leading parts anywhere—in rubbishy scripts, if need be—but play leading parts.

I'm not competitive. I don't think of stardom or acting as a sort of competition. Montgomery Clift once said that jealousy of another actor was the highest compliment you could pay him. Clift thought it was healthy to loathe another actor for his performance because it was like saying, "I wish I'd done that." I don't advise actors to see things that way. It's self-destructive. If you're competitive and you're not always on a winning streak, you'll get bitter. Actually, I'm really quite vain about the whole problem because I figure there *is* no competition—I am what I am, and either I am needed as that or I'm not suitable anyway.

But feeling secure doesn't make me immune to reverence for certain great names in the business. When I was making *The Swarm*, my character had to deliver a lecture on survival to an assembled group at a missile base near Houston, Texas. I was in mid-speech when I suddenly became aware of the audience listening to me: Henry Fonda, Olivia de Havilland, Fred MacMurray, Richard Widmark. I dried stone dead. These weren't actors; they were legends. I rarely dry up, but being in the presence of all that film history, that was too much for me.

As I look to my future in this industry, eventually I would like to direct, but not quite yet. A director starts working on a picture three months before it starts shooting and continues working on it four months after shooting has ended. In the period a director needs to make one film, someone like myself, who acts in pictures a great deal, could have made four. So one reason for my not directing is simple: money.

And all in all, I think I'll know when to give up acting and start directing because to me it's easy to tell if you're still a star or if you're on the way down. If I'm a star, I get a script and they say, "We know it's about an Australian dwarf, but we'll change it a bit." If I'm on the way down, they'd say I was too short to play in *The Michael Caine Story*. Maybe then I'll direct.

EDUCATING RITA
Directed by Lewis Gilbert.   Columbia, 1983.

MICHAEL CAINE
FILMOGRAPHY

1956 **A HILL IN KOREA**
Directed by Julian Amyes   British Lion

1957 **HOW TO MURDER A RICH UNCLE**
Directed by Nigel Patrick   Columbia

1958 **ROOM 43**
Directed by Alvin Rakoff   Gaumont British

1958 **CARVE HER NAME WITH PRIDE**
Directed by Lewis Gilbert   Rank

1958 **BLIND SPOT**
Directed by Peter Maxwell   Butcher's

1958 **THE KEY**
Directed by Carol Reed   Columbia/Open Road

1959 **THE TWO-HEADED SPY**
Directed by André de Toth   Columbia

1960 **THE BULLDOG BREED**
Directed by Robert Asher   Rank

1960 **FOXHOLE IN CAIRO**
Directed by John Moxey   British Lion

1961 **THE DAY THE EARTH CAUGHT FIRE**
Directed by Val Guest   British Lion/Pax

1962 **SOLO FOR SPARROW**
Directed by Gordon Flemyng   Independent

1962 **WRONG ARM OF THE LAW**
Directed by Cliff Owen   Continental

1963 **ZULU**
Directed by Cy Endfield   Embassy

1965 **THE IPCRESS FILE**
Directed by Sidney J. Furie   Universal

1966 **THE WRONG BOX**
Directed by Bryan Forbes   Columbia

1966 **ALFIE**
Directed by Lewis Gilbert   Paramount

1966 **GAMBIT**
Directed by Ronald Neame   Universal

1966 **FUNERAL IN BERLIN**
Directed by Guy Hamilton   Paramount

1966 **HURRY SUNDOWN**
Directed by Otto Preminger   Paramount

1967 **TONIGHT LET'S ALL MAKE LOVE IN LONDON**
Directed by Peter Whitehead   Gaumont British

1967 **BILLION DOLLAR BRAIN**
Directed by Ken Russell   United Artists

1967 **WOMAN TIMES SEVEN**
Directed by Vittorio de Sica   Embassy

1968 **THE MAGUS**
Directed by Guy Green   20th Century-Fox

1968 **DEADFALL**
Directed by Bryan Forbes   20th Century-Fox

1968 **PLAY DIRTY**
Directed by André de Toth   United Artists

1969 **THE ITALIAN JOB**
Directed by Peter Collinson   Paramount

1969 **THE BATTLE OF BRITAIN**
Directed by Guy Hamilton   United Artists

1969 **TOO LATE THE HERO**
Directed by Robert Aldrich   ABC/Cinerama

1970 **THE LAST VALLEY**
Directed by James Clavell   ABC/Cinerama

1971 **GET CARTER**
Directed by Michael Hodges   MGM

1971 **X, Y & ZEE**
Directed by Brian G. Hutton   Columbia

1971 **KIDNAPPED**
Directed by Delbert Mann   AIP

1972 **PULP**
Directed by Michael Hodges   United Artists

1972 **SLEUTH**
Directed by Joseph L. Mankiewicz   20th Century-Fox

1974 **THE DESTRUCTORS**
Directed by Robert Parrish   AIP

1974 **THE BLACK WINDMILL**
Directed by Don Siegel   Universal

1974 **THE WILBY CONSPIRACY**
Directed by Ralph Nelson   United Artists

1975 **PEEPER**
Directed by Peter Hyams   20th Century-Fox

1975 **THE ROMANTIC ENGLISHWOMAN**
Directed by Joseph Losey   Independent

1975 **THE MAN WHO WOULD BE KING**
Directed by John Huston   Allied Artists

1975 **THE EAGLE HAS LANDED**
Directed by John Sturges   Columbia

1976 **HARRY AND WALTER GO TO NEW YORK**
Directed by Mark Rydell   Columbia

1977 **A BRIDGE TOO FAR**
Directed by Richard Attenborough   United Artists

1978 **SILVER BEARS**
Directed by Ivan Passer   Columbia

1978 **THE SWARM**
Directed by Irwin Allen   AIP/Warner Brothers

1978 **CALIFORNIA SUITE**
Directed by Herbert Ross   Columbia

1979 **ASHANTI**
Directed by Richard Fleischer   Warner Brothers

1979 **BEYOND THE POSEIDON ADVENTURE**
Directed by Irwin Allen   Warner Brothers

1980 **THE ISLAND**
Directed by Michael Ritchie   Universal

1980 **DRESSED TO KILL**
Directed by Brian de Palma   AIP/Filmways

1981 **THE HAND**
Directed by Oliver Stone   Warner Bros./Orion

1981 **VICTORY**
Directed by John Huston   Paramount

1982 **DEATHTRAP**
Directed by Sidney Lumet   Warner Brothers

1983	**EDUCATING RITA** Directed by Lewis Gilbert	Columbia
1983	**BEYOND THE LIMIT** Directed by John MacKenzie	Paramount
1983	**THE JIGSAW MAN** Directed by Terence Young	Independent
1983	**BLAME IT ON RIO** Directed by Stanley Donen	20th Century-Fox
1985	**WATER** Directed by Dick Clement	HandMade Films
1985	**THE HOLCROFT COVENANT** Directed by John Frankenheimer	Universal
1985	**HANNAH AND HER SISTERS** Directed by Woody Allen	Orion
1985	**SWEET LIBERTY** Directed by Alan Alda	Universal
1986	**HALF-MOON STREET** Directed by Bob Swaim	20th Century-Fox
1986	**MONA LISA** Directed by Neil Jordan	Island Pictures
1986	**THE WHISTLE BLOWER** Directed by Simon Langton	Independent
1986	**THE FOURTH PROTOCOL** Directed by John MacKenzie	Lorimar
1987	**SURRENDER** Directed by Jerry Belson	Warner Brothers
1987	**JAWS: THE REVENGE** Directed by Joseph Sargent	Universal
1988	**WITHOUT A CLUE** Directed by Thom Eberhardt	Orion
1988	**DIRTY ROTTEN SCOUNDRELS** Directed by Frank Oz	Orion
1990	**A SHOCK TO THE SYSTEM** Directed by Jan Egleson	Corsair Pictures
1990	**BULLSEYE!** Directed by Michael Winner	21st Century Productions

EDITOR'S NOTE

This book was taken in part from the transcript of Michael Caine's views as he expressed them in his two-day recorded class on acting in film produced for television by Dramatis Personae Ltd. in conjunction with the BBC.

Acting in Film, the video, is one of a series of master classes showing practical acting techniques. Each episode relates to a particular medium (e.g. opera or film) or a particular type of drama (e.g. Restoration Comedy or farce). Each class is led by a recognized master of the genre. Scripted scenes are discussed and rehearsed by the master with a small group of actors. An invited audience observes the evolution of the work and has the opportunity to ask questions. Videos of the Acting Series Programs are available and are intended to be consulted either separately or together with the books.

Thanks must first go to Michael Caine, the master of *Acting in Film* and the class he led. The class included the talented British actors Simon Cutter, Celia Imrie, Mark Jefferies, Ian Redford, and Shirin Taylor. The producers for Dramatis Personae were myself and Nathan Silver, my partner. Our BBC co-producer and the program's director, providing every skill we lacked, was David G. Croft. Special thanks to National Film Archive London, Theo Cowan, and Jerry Pam. Glenn Young of Applause Theatre Books, our publisher, had the vision to see that the series ought to be done in individual books/videos and gave invaluable editing advice.

Maria Aitken

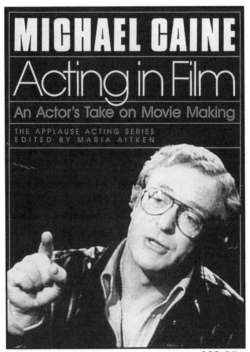